I0170453

At the End of the Day

**Essays
From an Award-Winning
Alzheimer's Blog
earlyonset.blogspot.com**

By

L. S. Fisher

MoZark

www.MozarkPress.com

All rights reserved. This book may not be reproduced in whole or in part or transmitted in any form without written permission by the publisher, except by a reviewer who may quote brief passages in a review; nor may any part of this book be reproduced, stored in a retrieval system, or transmitted in any form or by any means electronic, mechanical, photocopying, recording, or other without written permission from the publisher.

© August 2016 Linda Fisher

Published by Mozark Press, www.Mozarkpress.com
PO Box 1746, Sedalia, MO 65302

Cover Photo: "At the End of the Day" by Linda Fisher

Acknowledgement: Cover design and book layout by H.D. Ream

DISCLAIMER: *Statements or opinions expressed in the stories and articles of this publication are those of the author and do not necessarily represent the views or positions of any person or entity associated with publication of the book or the Alzheimer's Association.*

ISBN: 978-0-9903270-2-8

Dedication

Early Onset Alzheimer's Blog is dedicated to Jimmy D. Fisher and to all whose lives have been disrupted by a debilitating disease and to their families.

Other Titles by L. S. Fisher

Alzheimer's Anthology of
Unconditional Love

Early Onset Blog
Essays from an Online Journal
(Ozark Writers League 2010 Book of the Year)

Early Onset Blog
The Friendship Connection and Other Essays

Early Onset Alzheimer's
Encourage, Inspire, and Inform

Early Onset Alzheimer's
My Recollections, Our Memories

Focus on the Positive

Garden of Hope

The Broken Road

Available at www.lsfisher.com

Table of Contents

Introduction

One thing I learned as a primary caregiver was that the end of the day had its own special challenges. As I was winding down, Jim was revving up.

This behavior problem, known as sundowning, is common. Jim's pacing, agitation, and confusion seemed to escalate throughout the day and into the night. Sleep became a precious commodity at our house.

After I placed Jim into long-term care, the end of the day could still be a challenge. Almost daily, I left work and instead of heading home, drove to the care facility to spend time with Jim. He ate better when I fed him. I had a much easier time bathing him than staff. And most of all, I rested easier after I had personally checked on him and knew he had eaten and was comfortably tucked into bed.

Taking care of another human being is hard. In my opinion, the physical part of caregiving is not as difficult as the emotional grief. Perhaps the hardest of all for me was to stay positive and maintain my own physical and mental health.

My decisions as a caregiver were not perfect, but at the end of the day, I felt my most important job was to do the best I could.

Throughout the progression of Jim's disease, my litmus test was whether the decisions I made were the best ones under the circumstances. Sure, I could have second-guessed myself into the next year, but sometimes I had to be decisive. Often, my final decision was based on input from my two sons and Jim's mom. The four of us would often consider what we thought Jim would have wanted if he had been able to make his own decision.

Jim's life wasn't defined by dementia. He lived forty-nine years dedicated to his family, generous to a fault, sensitive, mystical at times, and from childhood played any instrument with strings. He lived a normal life without an inkling that his personality traits and skills could be slowly erased by a disease.

Through my blog, I celebrate Jim's life and try to encourage others traveling the Alzheimer's journey, inspire people to join in the fight against Alzheimer's, and provide information about the disease, research, and best caregiving practices.

I want my blog to have substance, but add a touch of humor from time to time. My goal in publishing my online journal is to reach more people with a message that each day is to be treasured. We all get discouraged, but by digging deep into our indomitable spirits, we can conquer the difficulties life throws our way.

At the end of the day, all we can do is take excellent care of our loved ones with dementia and put an end to this awful disease. In the meantime, my wish is that each of us lives life to the fullest!

~ Linda Fisher

A New Year's Revolution to End Alzheimer's

This is the beginning of a new year, and I think it's time we organize a revolution against Alzheimer's disease. The National Alzheimer's Plan is to find a prevention or effective cure for Alzheimer's by 2025. When I woke up this morning, I realized that is only ten years from now!

Ten years may seem like a long time, but it isn't. It takes an average of twelve years for a drug to traverse the path from research lab to the patient. Ninety percent of the drugs in preclinical testing are never tested on humans. Of the ones that make it to human testing only one in five will ever be approved.

So what can you do to join the revolution? Assuming you are not a researcher, your efforts can be focused in a different way. You can join the battle to End Alzheimer's!

1. Contact your legislators. Write letters, make phone calls, send emails, or visit them in district or D.C. The government funnels research dollars through the National Institutes of Health (NIH). NIH annually submits a budget request, which after modification is submitted to Congress from the president. Alzheimer's research is underfunded at $480 million.* In June, thanks to advocacy efforts, an additional $100 million was added to the NIH budget. To put this in perspective, NIH spends $6 billion (with a *B*) on cancer research, $4 billion on heart disease, and $3 billion on HIV/AIDS research annually. Researchers use grants to develop treatments. Do the math.

2. Participate in Walk to End Alzheimer's. More than 450,000 participants in 600 walks nationwide raised awareness and funds for Alzheimer's care, support, and research. The Alzheimer's Association is the largest nonprofit funder of Alzheimer's research and the world's leading voluntary health organization for Alzheimer's care.

3. Contact your local chapter. The Alzheimer's Association has 70 chapters that serve communities across the United States. Chapters are the frontlines in the battle against Alzheimer's. They will help you find the resources you need to navigate through the quagmire of living with Alzheimer's.

4. Arm yourself! No one goes into battle without equipment, ammunition, and a plan. To prepare yourself, acquire knowledge about the disease and develop a plan that will provide quality of life for the person with the disease and the care partner. Learn how to communicate and alleviate the stress caused by behavior.

5. Build a support system. Surround yourself with friends, family, and loved ones who will support you. You need people that will be on your side even when the going gets rough. Build a medical team for the person with dementia and the care partner—primary physician, neurologist, and specialists in any other illnesses such as diabetes, heart disease, cancer.

6. Keep a log of all medical information. Use pen and paper, a document, spreadsheet—whatever works for you—detailing all treatments, medications, side effects, tests. This will help you fill out medical forms and avoid unnecessary tests or medications that caused side effects.

7. **Enjoy life!** Watch for moments of joy and don't stop living. Don't place everything on hold. Alzheimer's is a disease that can last for decades. Learn to adapt to each stage and pursue activities that put a smile on your face. Love and patience overcome a lot of barriers.

More than five million people in the United States currently have Alzheimer's disease and new cases are skyrocketing. Alzheimer's is the sixth leading cause of death and the only disease in the top ten without an effective treatment or cure. *No* cure. A hundred percent fatal.

Where is the outcry? The outrage? This country has never been one to sit on its hands and let a disease wipe out millions of people—but that is exactly what is happening with Alzheimer's.

That is why it's time for a revolution. This disease, and related dementias—vascular dementia, Lewy body dementia, frontotemporal degeneration, mixed dementia, Parkinson's, Creutzfeldt-Jakob, normal pressure hydrocephalus, the rare dementias (including corticobasal degeneration)—has to stop. NOW. It is time to arm ourselves with passion and knowledge to eradicate Alzheimer's disease once and for all. Won't you become an advocate and join the fight to End Alzheimer's?

*Note: Alzheimer's funding was increased by an additional $350 million for FY 2016 due to advocacy efforts.

Baby, It's Cold Outside

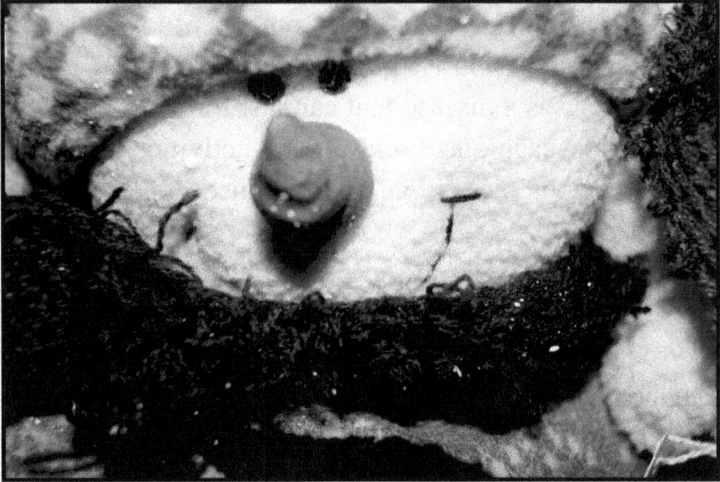

According to my phone, this morning the temperature was hovering at a balmy nine degrees and a cyclonic wind pushed the "real feel" way below zero. My last therapy appointment was today at 11:00 a.m. I dreaded going outside and would have loved to burrow under the covers and drink coffee. But, dang, I couldn't miss my last appointment.

At least I was geared up for it to be my last one. I was a little concerned, because Monday, as I entered the school to watch my granddaughter play basketball, I tripped on the threshold. My right shoe came off and I landed splat on the floor a short nanosecond later. Holy cow, to add insult to injury, I landed on the very arm I had been working on in therapy.

After the initial pain and agony, I spent some quality hours on a heat pad. I downed some ibuprofen and didn't feel too bad on Tuesday, my day off from therapy. By this morning, I was ready to give it a whirl.

Which brings me back to the weather. I layered my clothing and put on my heaviest coat before I headed out the door. When I got to Peak Performance, the parking lot was much emptier than I'd ever seen it. Sure enough, they had a lot of cancellations. After my therapy, I headed home. It was too darned cold to do anything else.

Cold weathers seems to breed misery. There's nothing that says "Big Chill" like frozen water pipes or a car that won't start. I remember the days when we drove an old vehicle, and Jim would get up every few hours during the night to start it up so that we would be able to go to work.

Every summer we complain about how hot it is outside, but when winter hits, we decide that the heat of summer wasn't so bad after all. There's nothing like getting hit with an icy north wind to make you long for the dog days of summer.

This frigid winter weather can be hazardous to life and limb. The weather advisory on my phone warned of frostbite and hypothermia. During a cold snap in November, two homeless men died in our town. I can't even imagine how frightening it would be to be homeless when wind chills are expected to be twenty below zero.

These temperatures are also dangerous for people with dementia. Seventy percent of individuals with dementia wander. While this is a concern in decent weather, severely cold weather presents a real and imminent danger. Even dressed for the weather, time outside must be limited. Too often people with dementia wander off without a coat, hat, and gloves.

Cold weather isn't too bad in a well-insulated house. When we lived in a mobile home, water froze overnight in a cup I had left in the sink. We'd crank the heat up as high as it would go, but the furnace couldn't compete with the wind whistling around poorly installed windows and doors.

I feel for people who live in older homes that are not well insulated. Another time we lived in an older home and the propane lines froze. We sent the kids to their grandma and grandpa's house while we tried to get the furnace working again and keep the water from freezing. I remember us huddling under a blanket using a hair dryer to generate heat. If that happened now, I'd probably check into a hotel until the spring thaw.

I shouldn't complain too much about the cold while I'm warm and cozy. Not everyone can keep warm in this type of weather and that bothers me.

Yes, baby, it's cold outside, but better days are coming. I guess the cheery thought is—spring is only seventy-one days away.

Has Stanford Found a Cure for Alzheimer's?

It is with optimistic caution that I share the latest good news regarding Alzheimer's research from Stanford University. They may have found the elusive and overdue cure for Alzheimer's disease. Over the past fifteen years, I've heard exciting news about Alzheimer's research that fizzled out after sailing through preliminary testing.

Is the Stanford University research going to be exception to past experience? I hope so!

I've always heard that you can't keep doing the same thing and expect a different outcome. That is one reason that grants are often awarded to researchers who try a new approach to the same problem: *What causes Alzheimer's and how can it be cured?*

The hallmarks of Alzheimer's disease are deposits of beta-amyloid plaques between nerve cells and tangles of the protein tau that build up inside cells. Aging is the number one risk factor for developing the disease, but it is not a normal part of aging.

Alzheimer's, a destructive and always fatal brain disease, is currently the sixth leading cause of death in the United States. Alzheimer's relentlessly progresses from mild symptoms to the final stages requiring constant care. People with the disease live an average of eight years, but some live twenty years or longer.

Stanford's approach is to boost the brain's own immune response to prevent and cure Alzheimer's. Researchers at Stanford University School of Medicine discovered that by blocking the protein EP2, microglia cells will continue to cleanse the brain of dangerous beta-amyloid deposits.

"The microglia are supposed to be, from the get-go, constantly clearing amyloid-beta, as well as keeping a lid on inflammation," Dr. Katrin Andreasson, professor of neurology and neurological sciences at Stanford, said.

Microglia cells are your own personal defense system. Their function is to search and destroy dead cells and other debris in the brain such as the gummy deposits Alzheimer's disease leaves in the wake of its destructive path.

Experiments on mice have been encouraging. Microglia goes about its business of protecting the brains of young mice. In older mice, the presence of EP2 proteins stopped the microglia cells from doing their job of destroying the dead cells. Another group of mice were genetically engineered to never develop EP2, and even when injected with beta-amyloid did not develop Alzheimer's. News that is even more exciting for people with Alzheimer's—blocking EP2 in older mice reversed the memory loss!

Of course, a great distance separates animal testing and drug development. Stanford has hopes of developing a drug to block EP2. They believe a compound that only blocks EP2 would not have unnecessary side effects.

Have researchers finally found the key to unlock the mystery of Alzheimer's disease? Time will tell if the Stanford study is the long-awaited breakthrough and the end of Alzheimer's.

Live until You Die

Recently Harold and I went on a fifteen-day cruise to Hawaii with my brother, his wife, my sister, and her husband. While at our last port, Kona, my brother said, "I saw something today that I've never seen before on a cruise." Since he is the most seasoned "cruiser" in our family, this statement surprised me.

"I saw them load a body on the boat this morning." He went on to say a hearse came to the pier and picked up the body.

"At least he was living when he died," my sister-in-law said. "It's a heck of a lot better than laying around in a nursing home waiting to die."

This made me think about something that my mother said several years ago after Jim developed dementia. She said, "I'm sure glad you and Jim didn't put off traveling until retirement." So was I, since retirement was never meant to be for us. Travel, we did! Mostly we traveled west—Oregon, Colorado, Utah, Idaho, and New Mexico. In addition, we expanded our journeys by going south, north, and east—sometimes vacations and, other times, on business trips.

The important thing is that we lived. Jim always said planning a trip gave him "something to look forward to." His lifestyle growing up was that of a vagabond. Getting in the car and heading out to a new territory meant adventure. A new day, a new experience. When the Fisher family returned to a locale, it was a sense of returning "home" to reunite with friends, family, or the weeping willow tree that grew in the front yard of a house where they once lived. Either way he was happy. He was living. He had many "homes" that resided in his memory and heart.

I, on the other hand, grew up living in one house in a remote area of the Missouri Ozarks. Travel was not something we did. Until my senior trip, I had only been out of state one time.

Other than the difference in our traveling experience, Jim and I had a lot in common. We both came from big families without many material possessions, parents that remained married until death, relatives that played guitars and sang country music, and a love of family. We both grew up with cousins as our best friends and playmates.

Eventually, we found our groove—living in one area to satisfy me, but traveling to satisfy Jim. Even after Jim was diagnosed with dementia and traveling became a different kind of adventure, we still managed to revisit the familiar, Colorado and Branson, and to experience new locales, Maine and Nova Scotia. We continued to live.

If there's one thing I've figured out from our journey into dementia, it is that living is a choice. When you consider the long-term scope of the disease, the choice to make the best of the time remaining seems more important than ever.

Don't waste the time you are given in the early stages of the disease. As the disease progresses, adapt. An adventure may be as simple as a trip to the park, or Dairy Queen for a milkshake, or taking a wheelchair for a spin around the parking lot.

I can't think of anything more heart wrenching than watching a loved one's emotions, memories, and skills deteriorate, but the one thing you have is the gift of time. Although it may seem that time is not your friend when you reach the later stages, it is a gift that people often do not have. Clutch and cherish those moments. Choose to live until you die.

Alzheimer's: The Triple Threat

Alzheimer's disease is a looming threat to each of us and to our government. In fact, it is a triple threat.

Threat #1: Soaring Prevalence. Every 67 seconds a person in the United States develops Alzheimer's. More than five million Americans currently are living with the disease. As the baby boomers age, the prevalence of Alzheimer's will skyrocket. Left unchecked, we could be looking at 16 million people with the disease by 2050. Don't know about you, but that darn near scares the bejesus out of me.

Threat #2: Lack of Treatment. Alzheimer's is the sixth leading cause of death in the United States. It is the only disease in the top ten without an effective treatment or a cure. We seem to be headed in the right direction with the Alzheimer's Accountability Act, which means the research budget is scientist driven. The goal is to move toward the National Alzheimer's Plan and find an effective treatment or a cure by 2025. Some recent studies are promising!

Threat #3: Enormous Costs. Alzheimer's has a reputation for being the most expensive disease for a reason. It is! The cost to Medicaid is $37 billion and Medicare is $113 billion, or one in five Medicare dollars. I can't quite wrap my mind around those staggering numbers.

Families provide an estimated 17.7 billion hours of unpaid care. In 2014, the out of pocket expense to American families to care for loved ones with Alzheimer's was estimated to be $36 billion. Additional costs hit family budgets hard. Even with health insurance and a division of assets that meant Medicaid picked up part of Jim's nursing home, the disease drained our resources. Jim's veteran's check and social security check went to the nursing home. The extras I bought for him cost much more than the $25 a month allowance from his checks.

When faced with a threat, humans have an instinct of either "flight" or "fight." Which do you have? If you fall into the "flight" camp, you ignore the disease and figure it isn't going to happen to you or someone you love. You don't bother to do anything about it. Maybe it's not because you don't care, but you don't have the time, money, or motivation.

If you are like me, you plan to "fight" with all you have. You walk the walk and talk the talk. You participate in Walk to End Alzheimer's, or at least support someone who does, and you become an advocate. You spread the word and email a legislator from time to time. You become a "Voice" for Alzheimer's.

Last night I listened in on an ambassador call, "Changing the Trajectory of Alzheimer's Disease." The moderators mentioned three ways to help us move the Alzheimer's mission forward. They called them the three "F's."

First, we need Fighters! These are the champions who visit, email, call, and generally pester their legislators about Alzheimer's legislation. They are ambassadors, board members, and volunteers who faithfully give their time and resources.

Second, we need Faces. A personal story, a picture, or a person in front of a legislator takes the abstract and makes it a reality! Whether you are visiting your state or U.S. legislators, the most important thing you can bring as an advocate is your story to make it personal and real. You need to condense the story to keep it on point and brief, but tell it from the heart.

The third part is to share the Facts. The facts are scary! The facts are sobering. You don't have to memorize the facts, but you need to share them. The best way to lay out the facts is to verbalize a few key facts and leave a handout behind with the details.

We have our work cut out for us if we intend to neutralize the triple threat of Alzheimer's and change the trajectory of the disease. I hope you choose to join the fight.

Memory Day Common Sense Proposals

On a cold February morning, Ginger and I joined other Missouri advocates for Memory Day at the state Capitol. With the temperatures in the teens and wind chills below zero, we made the trek from the parking garage to the Capitol building basement. That was a great place to enter the building since the cafeteria was close by and a hot cup of coffee helped take off the chill.

I found my cousin, Karen, and her lobbying partner at what they called their "office." This was a perfect area to see everyone entered the building. Ginger and I joined them, and while we enjoyed our coffee, we received our first lucky break of the day. My cousin had a place for us to leave our coats. How great to not have to lug them around.

"Usually when we get here," I told her, "we have this big discussion as to whether it's cold enough that we have to wear our coats. That wasn't an option this morning."

Soon, the Alzheimer's group passed by, and we discovered that we were now meeting in Hearing Room #2, instead of #3. We would meet to receive our appointment schedules, leave behind packets, instructions, and don our purple sashes. Our Springfield group was unable to come because of ice, so our group was smaller than usual.

The Memory Day ceremony had been moved to 2:00 p.m., so for the first time, we had lunch first. Better yet, we weren't rushed!

Another first: Ginger and I had different representatives. Since I'd moved a few miles down the road, I was in a new district.

We had two important issues to discuss with our legislators.

Alzheimer's Grants. We have been fortunate to receive Alzheimer's service grants for many years. This year we asked for $450,000 to be budgeted for grants to provide respite care for Missourians with Alzheimer's or a related dementia. This grant has the potential to save the state millions each year. How is that possible?

Respite often helps caregivers keep loved ones at home longer. Eight hundred families receive respite from this grant. Nursing home care costs Medicaid (paid by the state) an average of $147 per day. Sixty percent of nursing home residents are on Medicaid. If respite funds delay nursing home placement for Medicaid eligible persons by one month (30 days), the state would save $2,116,800. The savings alone makes sense! I delayed nursing home placement by several months with in-home care partially paid with respite funds. It is impossible to place a value on how much that time meant to us.

Senior Savings Protection Act (SB 244/HB 636). We all know how on our toes we have to be to avoid being scammed. People with dementia are even more vulnerable to being exploited. This bill would allow financial industry professionals to reach out to state agencies and family members if they suspect senior clients are being exploited and to refuse disbursements up to ten days. Folks, this is so necessary! Jim had me to run interference for him when telemarketers and others tried to take advantage of him. Not everyone has a person who can keep track of all the unscrupulous shysters out there who would love nothing better than to tap someone's bank account.

Our first scheduled visit was to see Ginger's representative, Rep. Dave Muntzel, who until August had been mine. After our visit with him, we went directly to visit Rep. Dean Dohrman, my representative. Both representatives seemed to understand the value of both respite funds and the senior protection bill.

After these visits, we split up. Ginger went to the ceremony, and I accompanied another advocate on his legislative visit. As soon as our meeting ended, we walked to the second floor rotunda area where Lt. Governor Peter Kinder was talking about Alzheimer's impact on families and government. Advocates held flowers representing their connection to the disease. The program ended with a caregiver's personal story.

I dropped off a packet for our senator and retrieved our coats. On the drive back to Sedalia, Ginger and I talked about the day, our impressions, our hopes and fears. It had been a tiring day, but productive.

Being an advocate means being a voice. Each of us can be a voice to help advance these important issues in Missouri. Face-to-face meetings make the most difference, but you can lend your support with a letter, phone call, or email. It only takes a moment, but approval of the $450,000 Alzheimer's Grant could be a lifeline for someone you love and save the state millions at the same time. The Senior Savings Protection Act could help your grandparents or elderly parents keep their hard-earned savings. These two issues are a win-win for Missouri residents and taxpayers.

A Box of Memories

Last week I opened a box of photos and found a hodgepodge of memories packed inside. I had stashed miscellaneous photos in this box, and the memories spanned decades, *many* decades.

I started sorting the loose photos into labeled envelopes with hopes that eventually I could find a specific photo when I wanted. I began the task of labeling photos and trying to date them. Some were still in the envelopes from the various places where I had them developed. Although I didn't take the time to label the photos, I often put the place and year on the outside. As I shuffled through them, I was reminded of happy times, family reunions, vacations, and get-togethers.

I was searching for a photo for an Alzheimer's presentation I'm giving this weekend, and in addition to the box, I sifted through thousands of photos on my computer. I was amazed at how many of the digital photos I didn't remember taking.

I've finally started organizing my digital photos by putting them in folders by subject and by year. It does make it easier to find that one photo I'm looking for to jog a memory, savor a moment, or for a brief wallow in nostalgia.

As I've gotten older, I've discovered how important it is to have these mementos. Too many people are gone before we're ready. Too often family moves across country and our paths won't cross for years or decades at a time. Or maybe we won't meet again on this side of heaven.

Rare old photographs are meant to be enjoyed and shared. Poor families have fewer photos than wealthier ones. You not only had to buy a camera, you had to purchase film, and then pay to have it developed. Sometimes the process took months if you hadn't taken the entire roll of film. Or, you'd put it aside and forgot to have the photos developed. When that happened, photos often had a strange cast to them. It seemed like in every group photo at least one person was looking away, talking, or had her eyes shut.

I know my mother-in-law lost a lot of her family photos in a fire. Those irreplaceable images are gone forever.

What a different world it was then. My hairdresser and I were talking about the numerous "selfies" people take today. She was wondering why her daughter had to have so many pictures of herself.

Well, let's face it. The younger you are, the better the photos turn out. At my age, I prefer to have my hair fixed and my makeup on. It doesn't help to be dressed in something that makes me look like a baby elephant. It's hard to look trim in photos when you aren't in real life. But let's face it—there are good photos and not so good ones.

This morning when I was organizing some of my digital photos, I saw one Harold took of me with my new camera. I didn't have a speck of makeup on, and in high quality digital, you can see every flaw on my face. I almost deleted it, and then decided what the heck; it wouldn't look bad at all with a little Photoshop magic.

It is so easy to scan or take a photograph and share within seconds on Facebook. As I've uncovered some of the treasures in the box of pictures, my first thought was to share them with family members. I love looking at old photos others share on "Throwback Thursday." The photos make me smile—sometimes through tears—but a big smile, just the same.

I'm so glad that I have thousands of digital and prints of people, places, and memories. Photos are slices of life—precious moments frozen in time.

Alzheimer's Everywhere I Go

Last weekend, I had the privilege of speaking at the Business Women of Missouri legislative conference on Alzheimer's legislation. A women's group is an ideal audience for a topic of Alzheimer's. Two-thirds of those stricken with the disease are women. In addition, women are two times more likely to be the caregiver for a loved one with the disease.

Spouses and daughters make up the majority of the female care partners, but in younger onset, a mother may be a caregiver. In Jim's case, his mom took care of him while I worked. Her failing health and the progression of the disease left me scrambling for other relatives and professional caregivers. Bless my mom, sister, sons, and in-laws for being the village that helped me keep him at home longer.

It seems that everywhere I go, I run into others who know the heartbreak of Alzheimer's. Folks tend to share their experiences with me. Or their concerns. Often, I see the concern when the horrible suspicion takes hold that something is terribly wrong with a loved one. From my experience, I completely understand the urgency of wanting to find out what is wrong, and the fear that the doctor will say, "dementia" or "dementia of the Alzheimer's type."

First, before panic sets in, take your loved one for a complete medical and psychological workup. I believe that nothing would have been more devastating to me than to find out, too late, that something could have been done to help Jim, and we hadn't started proper treatment. Some treatable conditions can mimic Alzheimer's.

Also, psychological testing can measure the level of cognition. I was stunned to learn that Jim had dementia after a battery of psychological testing. Simple things baffled him: he couldn't count backwards from ten, he couldn't come up with any words that started with the letter *a*, and he couldn't perform simple math. Abstract thinking was beyond his capabilities.

Jim's follow-up MRI detected brain shrinkage. We ran out of other reasons for his problems.

Alzheimer's is an insidious disease. It sabotages lives and steals the future. It predictably moves throughout the brain, relentlessly destroying brain cells.

Caregivers can become frustrated when they hear the same question or phrase, repeatedly. They can become annoyed with repetitive behavior. Jim folded paper towels, dozens of them, and stuffed them into his pockets. He paced. And paced. And paced right out the door and down the road.

"It's just the disease," I told myself. I told others the same thing when they couldn't understand why Jim did some of the things he did. Knowing it's the disease, does help.

"If Jim had a broken leg, would people expect him to walk?" my mom reasoned. "Well, he has a broken brain, and no one can expect him to do the things he used to do."

When Jim was in the early stages of the disease, I think some people believed I was the problem. I saw little things, subtle changes that it took another year for others to see.

Now I see others beginning that journey, hoping it isn't Alzheimer's. They notice differences that may not be obvious to anyone else.

I don't know how many times I've heard, "Oh, my uncle doesn't have Alzheimer's! He can remember everything that happened when he was a boy."

Yes. We grasp at straws and hang onto denial for as long as possible. If he can't remember where the bathroom is in his own house, or drives to town and can't find his way home, or forgets his children's names, it's time to drop the denial and investigate.

We fear nothing as much as the unknown. And everywhere I go, I find people who begin to have that nagging doubt that gnaws at the pit of their stomachs, that someone they love is developing dementia. My heart aches for each of them. My prayers plead for them to be strong, because strong is the only choice if their fears become the ugly reality of Alzheimer's.

My hugs convey my hope that until science ends Alzheimer's they will make the most of the time they've been given. My dream is that someday, everywhere I go, I won't know anybody with Alzheimer's.

Spring into Action at the Alzheimer's Forum

Spring is finally here and I'm packing for my fifteenth annual trip to Washington, D.C. It's that time of year again when Alzheimer's advocates converge on Capitol Hill to deliver our message to Congress.

For the first time in several years, I'll be making the trip alone. My good friends Kathy and Sarah will be spending one night with me. We've never done that before, and I know it will be a blast with not much sleeping going on.

With the way my flights are, my free time is broken up into smaller chunks so I'm not sure how many of the wonderful historic sites I'll get to visit this time. Our hotel is in the Woodley Park area so we're quite a distance from the sites other than the Zoo. Of course, an entrance to the metro is a short distance away, so I imagine that will be my direct route to the monuments and museums.

Of course, I'm not there to be a tourist. I'm there to take on the serious business of advocating for Alzheimer's funding. Research news is really exciting right now.

Alzheimer's is a global problem and researchers are working worldwide to find a cure. A new study from Australia has shown reversal of Alzheimer's in animal models. Scientists used focused therapeutic ultrasound to beam noninvasive sound waves into the brain. This therapy worked on 75 percent of the mice, restoring memory, but not damaging surrounding tissue. That sounds totally awesome!

At least it's awesome for the mice, but folks, it makes you wonder how long it will be before it becomes available for our loved ones. This therapy will eventually be tried on "higher" animal models, such as sheep. Human trials could be underway as soon as 2017. These trials may start small, and perhaps, in Australia.

It's not surprising that this news comes from Australia. In 2004, they were the first country to adopt a national Alzheimer's plan. We didn't adopt our plan until eight years later.

Scientists are exploring several avenues now that show good results in mice ranging from a special diet to drugs that restore the immune system to normal so it can rid the brain of beta-amyloid plaque.

Research is costly, which brings me back to the reason to go to D.C. Our country is hard hit with Alzheimer's disease, which happens to be the most costly disease in America. Yet, we spend only one percent of the cost of the disease on research. We need to increase the investment in Alzheimer's research in order to meet our goal of a cure or effective treatment by 2025.

So my bag is packed and I leave early, early in the morning to make my flight. This time tomorrow, I'll be in D.C. preparing for a whirlwind of preparation for our Hill visits on Wednesday. We will spring into action and shout from the Hill: We want to *End Alzheimer's Now*.

Alzheimer's Advocacy Forum 2015

I joined 1,100 other focused and dedicated advocates in Washington, D.C., to take our message to Capitol Hill. As always, a highlight for me is to meet my long-term (fifteen years!) friends, and sisters of the heart, Sarah Harris and Kathy Siggins. This is the one time each year we get together, talking non-stop until we get caught up. Once we enter the forum, we're focused on the message.

The first training session for ambassadors began immediately following lunch on Monday. The program began with an exercise. Everyone was asked to shout his or her name. Of course, the result was a loud, indecipherable noise. Yet when everyone whispered in unison "Alzheimer's is the most expensive disease in America," it was easily understood. This demonstrated the impact of everyone being on the same page and delivering the same message.

Our mission was for Alzheimer's advocates to deliver our federal priorities to our senators and representatives.

1. Increase the commitment to Alzheimer's research by $300 million. The current level of investment is $586 million. Even with the increase, this amount is far short of the $2 billion annual estimate to implement the steps toward meeting the goal of a cure or effective treatment as set forth by the National Alzheimer's Plan.

2. Co-sponsor the Hope for Alzheimer's Act. During the Forum, the Act was re-introduced with a focus on care planning and documentation of medical records. This act is consistent with the National Alzheimer's Plan

The cost of caring for individuals with Alzheimer's is a staggering $226 billion. These numbers will only continue to increase as the baby boomers age. By 2050, the cost of Alzheimer's care is expected to reach $1.1 trillion per year. The only way to avoid this pending economic crisis is to find an effective treatment or cure for Alzheimer's disease.

Research today is exciting, and we seem to be on the cusp of finding the key to unlock the elusive cure for Alzheimer's. New studies have shown great promise. New technology allows scientists to see beta amyloid plaques and tau tangles in living brains. Now, the effectiveness of treatments can be measured through this imaging.

A breakout session on social media showed us how to use tools provided by the Association to share highlights of the session via social media—Twitter and Facebook. We participated in a "Thunderclap" that released hundreds of tweets and Facebook posts as we began our Hill visits. The Association also re-tweeted any tweets containing #ALZFORUM or #ENDALZ. During the National Alzheimer's Dinner, tweets were displayed on the screens, including several of mine.

All fifty states were represented during the roll call of the states. The most poignant moment during the roll call was an advocate accompanied by his wife who had Alzheimer's. My heart went out to both of them.

Dr. David Satcher, former U.S. Surgeon General presented the keynote. He focused on leadership and teamwork. "Everyone teaches and everyone learns," Dr. Satcher said. "Leadership is like a relay race." It doesn't just depend on how fast you run, but whether you have the baton at the finish line. "If you drop the baton, the race is over." He read a poem his wife, Nola, had written for their wedding reception, "I've Never Been Here Before." Nola was diagnosed with Alzheimer's fifteen years ago giving a new meaning to the poem.

Periodically, throughout the meeting, advocates and people with dementia would tell why they were advocates. The most delightful person to speak was Amy Shives. She said she was diagnosed at fifty, as was her mother, with dementia of the Alzheimer's type—atypical. She never considered herself to be typical anyway. She said that people with Alzheimer's did not like to be called "sufferers" because they are people, not the disease. "If you've met one person with Alzheimer's; you've met one person with Alzheimer's." Amy said that now she could wear her new shoes even if they don't match her dress. Her first dog, Chester, alerts her when she is going to have seizures. She freely admitted that her cat doesn't care. Her husband, George, is her care partner and she loves him more than ever. Amy is being considered for an appointment to next year's Alzheimer's Association Board of Directors.

Lisa Genova, author of *Still Alice*, received the Sargent and Eunice Shriver Profiles in Dignity Award. Lisa was at the 2008 Alzheimer's Forum speaking to an early stage group and selling her self-published book. I bought a book from Lisa during that long-ago Forum prepared to be disappointed. Boy, was I ever wrong! I was so impressed by *Still Alice* that when a student I was mentoring wanted to know what Alzheimer's book to review, I recommended *Still Alice*. The book was later published by Simon & Schuster. *Still Alice* spent forty weeks on the New York Times bestseller list and sold 2.1 million copies in thirty different languages. The movie, starring Julianne Moore, has followed a circuitous route to become an acclaimed movie co-produced by Elizabeth Gelfand Stearns, chair of the Judy Fund, who read the book in one night.

On Wednesday, we stormed Capitol Hill. Jessie Kwatamdia, Marcia Rauwerdink, and I along with other advocates visited Senator Blunt and Claire McCaskill's offices. We three then visited with Congresswoman Hartzler, where we received a warm reception.

After our visits, Jessie and I attended the senate hearing on the fight against Alzheimer's, Senator Susan Collins, chair, and Claire McCaskill, ranking member. Missouri advocate Kim Stemley, a young caregiver for her mother, gave a powerful, on-point testimony.

The influence of 1,100 dedicated advocates, wearing purple sashes, each delivering the same message, punctuated with personal stories, leaves a lasting impression on our legislators. Collectively, we are influential, but we are unstoppable as individuals who advocate throughout the year.

I am thankful to once again be part of this group and look forward to returning for my sixteenth Advocacy Forum April 4 – 6, 2016, to make sure our voices are not forgotten.

Unlikely Friends

You've always heard of fighting like dogs and cats, so Harold was concerned when the stray kitten showed up on our doorstep. It was a little worse for wear: tail torn off and bloody back legs. The kitten was dehydrated and hungry. What else can you do when a teeny kitten refuses to leave and sits there mewing much louder than you'd think possible?

Enter Neptune into the household ruled by Lucy. A short year before, Lucy had wormed her way into our hearts in the exact same manner—a stray who took up residence.

Harold was worried that Lucy wouldn't like the cat. I introduced them by letting them touch noses, and they had many staring contests. The cat stayed on the front porch, and Lucy was queen of the deck.

Cats being curious, Neptune eventually approached the deck. At first, the dog barked and Neptune backed away. That didn't last long. Soon Neptune was darting in front of Lucy and scooting behind the grill.

"The cat shouldn't be on the deck," Harold said as he shooed Neptune away. A few minutes later, the cat slid through the rail to venture onto the deck again.

After a few weeks, Lucy quit barking at the cat and they declared a truce. The cat took over Lucy's bed, and Lucy would lie beside it and nose Neptune. Sometimes they got a little rowdy, but neither seemed to be scared of the other.

While I was gone to the Alzheimer's Forum, Harold said, "The cat is going to have to go. They mock fight and one of them is going to get hurt." I don't believe he was worried so much about Lucy hurting Neptune as he was about Neptune scratching Lucy.

By the time I got home, he had to show me how they acted. When he took Lucy for a walk in the backyard, the cat went down the steps side-by-side with the dog. Then, the cat ran up a tree, only to sidle down and launch a sneak attack.

All was quiet when we were inside. On the surveillance camera, we saw them lying together on the same chair while four other chairs remained unoccupied. Now, Lucy prances about each morning anxious to go onto the deck to play with her unlikely friend.

It seems that throughout life, we all have unlikely friends. At the Forum each year, I look forward to spending quality time with my two friends, Kathy Siggins and Sarah Harris. It's an unlikely friendship when you consider that Sarah lives in Virginia, Kathy in Maryland, and I live in Missouri. Our friendship is never diminished from spending time away and when we meet at the Forum, we haven't missed a beat. The Forum is like a special homecoming of the heart.

We all lost our husbands to an Alzheimer's type of dementia. We met at the Forum and had an immediate connection. Now, it would be hard to imagine my life without them.

These serendipitous friendships are promises that nothing is random. No matter what happens, we will meet the people we are supposed to meet and fulfill the purpose we were born to accomplish.

"If it hadn't been for Alzheimer's," Sarah said, "we would have never met." This is an undeniable truth. Our adversities defined our strengths and shaped our souls allowing us to embrace our unlikely friendship.

Death and Taxes

April is a month that makes me think of death and taxes. April 15 came with alarming speed, and for the first time in a decade, I filed a joint return. Of course, we used a handy-dandy program to plug in the numbers. But what can I say, other than taxes are a little bit complicated. Bottom line turned up a shocking sum that I owed in taxes. Even paying what I thought was an unreasonable amount of quarterly estimated taxes throughout 2014; I wound up in debt to the IRS and to the state of Missouri.

Now, to prepare for the current year. Last year's estimated taxes were only about a third of this year's amount. Ouch! For all my complaints about taxes, I feel fortunate that I have a great retirement plan.

What is it they say about death and taxes? April is also the month that hurts my heart. Jim left this world April 18, ten years ago—a decade. It doesn't seem possible that it could be that long ago when I remember that day so plainly. Funny, how the more you want to forget something, the less likely you are to do it.

The only positive thing I can say about Jim's death is that it gave me back the man I knew before dementia. During the years struggling in the grip of the disease, it came to a point where the person he was faded, and he became a different person. In order to make it through that tough time, I refused to compare who he was to who he had been. It was easier to accept the unacceptable changes and love him "as is."

After Jim's death, I eventually was able to embrace the man he was before the disease. I could smile at old photos and memories before the dark days of dementia. I could remember our Colorado vacations, our trips to Oregon, and our big adventure of building our own home. So many good memories outweigh the sad times.

Life is a balance: good and bad, smiles and tears, joy and pain. You can't fully appreciate one without the other. If you were never sad, you wouldn't appreciate being happy. Part of the wonder of life is that we don't know what is going to happen the next day. Life can change in a heartbeat. Our world can turn upside down and it may take years, or decades, for it to righten again.

Ben Franklin said that death and taxes were the only two certain things in life. As for taxes, I guess, it means we do have income, and we can be thankful for that. It's hard to find much good to say about death, unless we can say we lived fully until that time. Jim lived fully until dementia made that impossible.

On April 18, I want to remember Jim's life and not his death. I want to remember his laugh, his corny jokes, and most of all, his loving heart.

What Is Alzheimer's Disease?

At the first Memory Walk I coordinated, a reporter from a local radio station placed a recorder beneath my chin, and asked, "What is Alzheimer's?" When he had asked for an interview, I expected him to ask what our financial goal was for the walk, why I was personally involved, what the money was used for, who our sponsors were, what it was like to be a caregiver, or even why purple was the "official" color. For some reason, it never occurred to me that he would ask me to define Alzheimer's disease.

I believe my answer was, "Alzheimer's is an incurable degenerative brain disease that affects memory and a person's ability to perform daily tasks."

Alzheimer's is not an easily defined disease. Even if you give a textbook, or dictionary, definition, it falls so far short of the scope of the disease that you might as well describe a malignant brain tumor as "a headache."

Yes, official definitions might give a clinical description that says "a general term for memory loss and other intellectual abilities serious enough to interfere with daily life." I'm not so sure that this disease "interferes with" daily life so much as it replaces life with a new reality. You go to a place where nothing is the way it had been, and you know it never will be the same.

It is important to know what Alzheimer's does to the brain; otherwise, you will expect the impossible. Without the knowledge that the brain is deteriorating, it is too easy to believe that someone is being willfully stubborn or "pretending" they cannot remember.

In 1906, Dr. Alois Alzheimer, a German psychiatrist and neuropathologist, had a fifty-one-year-old patient, Auguste Deter, who died after she exhibited odd behavior and suffered from memory loss. During the autopsy of her brain, Dr. Alzheimer discovered shrinking of the cortex, and the presence of amyloid plaques and neurofibrillary tangles. Amyloid plaques and tau tangles became the hallmark of Alzheimer's disease.

Most research centered on ways to rid the brain of amyloid plaques. More recently, researchers at Mayo Clinic have focused on tau. The study's lead author, Neuroscientist Melissa Murray, PhD, in *Brain* described the role of tau as "railroad ties that stabilize a train track that brain cells use to transport food, messages and other vital cargo throughout neurons." She described tau as "the driver of Alzheimer's."

As research moves closer to unlocking the mystery of Alzheimer's, it is important to note only 45 percent of those with Alzheimer's, or their caregivers, report being told of the diagnosis. This compares to 90 percent of people with cancer and cardiovascular disease knowing their condition.

Why is it so important to know of an Alzheimer's diagnosis since the disease is incurable and has no treatment to slow the progression? I know from experience that crucial decisions need to be made while the person with the disease can help make them. It is important to get finances in order and to put in place medical and financial durable power of attorney documents. Knowing the diagnosis will also help families connect with community resources.

Videos, books, and brochures explain how Alzheimer's affects the brain. To know how it affects lives and hearts, talk to a person with the disease or a caregiver. They are all too familiar with the daily challenges that truly define the disease.

The Alzheimer's Box

Several years ago, I went through piles of papers from my various volunteer organizations and threw them into different totes. This was a haphazard way of sorting them and was much quicker than making file folders and filing them away. Besides, at the time, my file space was quite limited so that may not have been an option.

Today, I sorted through the Alzheimer's tote. It was quite an interesting assortment of papers. The first task was to sort the papers into three piles: recycle, burn, and file. I quickly pared down the amount of information to keep to a smaller stack.

In the Alzheimer's box, I found articles that I thought were lost forever. I found the article about my friend, Karen Henley, published in *Newsday Magazine*. Karen was caring for her forty-two-year-old husband Mike, who had familial early-onset Alzheimer's disease. Her story is one of courage, perseverance, and most of all, love.

I found an article that made me smile. My friend, David Oliver, was one of the researchers who biked in the Alzheimer's Breakthrough Ride. I met him when we both served on the local Alzheimer's chapter board of directors. He had joined the cross-country ride (San Francisco to D.C.) for the segment from Sedalia to Jefferson City. I drove into town early for the send off. David and four others took the scenic route to Jefferson City. David was dedicated to go above and beyond to further Alzheimer's research funding. David passed away from cancer in March. It was especially touching to see this article and remember his wonderful sense of humor and optimistic outlook on life.

I found several years of *Advocate's Guides* and *Facts and Figures* from some of the fifteen Advocacy Forums I've attended over the years. I go through these two books each year to see what we've accomplished and what we need to tackle. They serve as a valuable resource for me.

Of course, I had several folders of Alzheimer's walks, previously known as "Memory Walks." I was able to pitch several old forms. At one time, we had to make our own! I spent hours developing signup sheets for team captains and posters for events. It's much easier now that the Alzheimer's Association and the chapter have everything online and with a few clicks, we can download and print any report, form, or poster we need.

Then to top it off, there's always the odd pieces of information. Prints of the airline tickets for one of the years my granddaughter went to D.C. with me. I found a stub from the Smithsonian and a map of the Old Town Trolley. I pitched an outdated congressional book.

Tucked in among the Alzheimer's papers were a few from Sedalia Business Women. Oops, guess that was in the wrong box entirely. That one is still intact. Who knows, when I go through it I might find more Alzheimer's memorabilia.

It's kind of sad to look back at years and years of events that have come and gone. I'm happy to say my passion for Alzheimer's advocacy is still alive. I'm looking forward to the day when it is no longer necessary and Alzheimer's is eradicated.

Alzheimer's Research—Climb the Highest Mountain

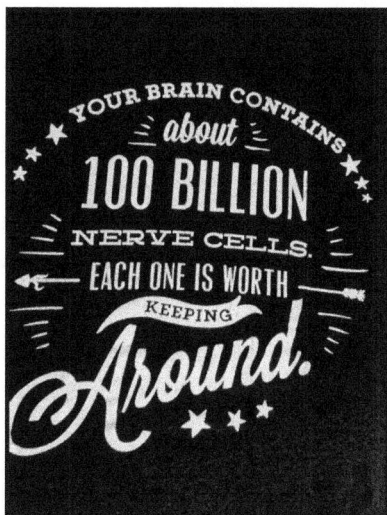

YOUR BRAIN CONTAINS
about
100 BILLION
NERVE CELLS.
EACH ONE IS WORTH
KEEPING
Around.

When you name your company after the highest mountain in North America, you know you have great expectations. A new company, Denali Therapeutics, has taken on the challenge of finding a cure for neurodegenerative diseases, including Alzheimer's. Their task is formidable, and that is the reason they chose Denali for their name.

The former Genetech researchers began their venture with an astounding $217 million. Denali's chairman of the board, Dr. Marc Tessier-Lavigne, believes that the time is right for breakthrough treatments for neurodegenerative diseases.

This group of scientists plans to break away from the study of drugs to block beta-amyloid. Their focus will be on genetics, which has led to effective drugs for cancer. Scientists have discovered new genes linked to brain diseases such as Alzheimer's, ALS, and Parkinson's. They believe these "degenogenes" will lead to a better outcome than previous drug studies.

Hallelujah! How often have you heard that if you keep trying the same thing you'll have the same outcome? Alzheimer's research is at an impasse. No one has found the illusive cure, or even a good treatment for the disease. It is time to try a complete new approach and these seem like just the guys to do it.

The company is looking at brain inflammation and the substances that develop between brain cells. They are concentrating on the factors that cause brain cells to die when a person develops a brain disease. They are already looking at twelve drug targets!

The brightest brains in the world have banded together to tackle the most baffling disease left to conquer. Now, they hope to engage the Food and Drug Administration in fast tracking brain drugs for Alzheimer's as they did for HIV and other diseases.

Today I'm wearing a T-shirt that says, "Your brain contains about 100 billion nerve cells. Each One Is Worth Keeping Around." I want to keep as many of those precious cells as I can. Don't you?

sources:
http://www.prnewswire.com/news-releases/denali-therapeutics-launches-with-initial-investment-to-discover-and-develop-treatments-for-neurodegenerative-diseases-300083259.html

http://www.forbes.com/sites/matthewherper/2015/05/14/former-genentech-researchers-raise-217-million-for-company-to-fight-alzheimers-and-parkinsons/

Four Reasons to Take a Leap of Faith

My granddaughter is on the track team of a small school that doesn't have their own track. When she decided to jump in addition to running, she watched a You-Tube video and practiced in the yard. It took a real leap of faith for her to try her skill at a track meet. Last year, she advanced to Sectional in the triple jump, and she was determined to do the same this year. At Districts this year, she placed third in triple jump and long jump.

A storm lurked behind dark clouds on the day of Sectionals. Her goal at Sectionals was to place in the top four and advance to State. After the long jump, she was disappointed because her jumps were short of her personal best, and it didn't look like she would advance. The skies opened up and a torrential rain sent us to the truck and her to the athletes' tent. After the downpour, she jumped the triple jump and, although she placed better than last year, she clearly wasn't in the top four.

She wasn't really open to hearing she'd done her best, or how proud of her we were, or "there's always next year." We left after her events and by the time we stopped in town for pizza, she was feeling better. Track season was over for the year. She'd had a great year, so her leap of faith to compete had paid off.

It got me to thinking about when a leap of faith is personally beneficial.

1. When failure, or even humiliation, is possible. When I decided to start my Early Onset Alzheimer's blog, doubts churned in my mind. Did I have anything of interest to say and would anyone read it? Would I have mistakes in it that people would criticize? Would I get hate mail? Negative images almost kept me from pushing the post button that first time. Once I made the decision to move forward, I never looked back. It is obvious that success is not possible without a chance of failure, and failure can be humiliating. It's moving beyond the fear that lets us know the thrill of accomplishing our goals.

2. To follow your dream. My dream was to write. Little did I know that when I was clacking out fiction stories on a manual typewriter, the future would hold many ways of publishing my work. Eventually, the time came when the mechanics of writing became about a thousand percent easier and publishing as easy as pushing the "post" button. Not everyone wants to be a writer, but almost everyone has a dream they want to follow. What's yours? Take a leap of faith and go for it!

3. Leave a dead end situation. We've all been there. The job that went nowhere. The relationship that caused more harm than good, or was downright scary. It is hard to leave the known for the unknown, but given the correct circumstances, it can be life changing. I once had a job working for a family business. It wasn't all bad, at first. I liked what I was doing but as the married couple's relationship went south, conditions became unbearable. I needed a job, so I stayed even after I began to dread going to work each day. I was forced into leaving the dead end situation when they sold the business. Thankfully, the demise of the company forced me into the job market and launched a life-long career at a job I loved.

4. Keep improbable from being impossible. I dropped out of college when I married Jim. Finally, when my children began school, I returned to our local junior college to earn a two-year degree. Still, I always regretted not getting my bachelor's degree, and the older I got, the more improbable it became that it was going to happen. The opportunity to get a degree came at a bad time. I was working full-time, Jim was in the nursing home, and I was already squeezing in time to volunteer for the Alzheimer's Association. Although the situation seemed impossible, I entered an eighteen-month cohort program offered by William Woods University. I graduated in 2005, easily the oldest student in our class. Was it worth it? You bet it was.

Taking a leap of faith doesn't always pan out, but not taking it strips you of the sweet taste of success.

Oh, during that downpour at the track meet, we missed the announcement of the long jump winners. My granddaughter's coach collected her medal and gave her the good news that evening: she had advanced to State. Will she win a medal at State? Maybe, maybe not, but without taking that leap of faith she would have never had the opportunity or experience.

Chasing after the Wind

Sometimes I'm in the right place at the right time to hear a message that resonates with me. That message may be at a high-priced conference in some exotic locale, or it could be in my hometown during one of Pastor Jim Downing's sermons.

Sunday morning, he prefaced his sermon with the thought that it might be one of the most important messages he would ever give. I don't remember his exact words, but he gave his self-depreciating smile, and said we might be thinking, "Nice words, preacher" and go on our way and side-step the importance of the message.

His message was based on Ecclesiastes 4:6 "Better one handful with tranquility than two handfuls with toil and chasing after the wind." We seem to think that more is better, but is it?

When I was growing up in a family of eight, we learned that it wasn't necessary to have a lot of material possessions to get by. Mom and Dad bought us school supplies and clothes at the beginning of the year. I had a few dresses to wear and one pair of school shoes. We always had the box of sixteen crayons, not the giant boxes some of the other kids had. Funny thing was, I still received the same education.

I had two dolls and not a lot of other toys. Mom always saw that I had books to read. She ordered a children's version of *Reader's Digest Condensed Books*. Through those books, the world of adventure opened to me. One of the first stories I read was "Little House in the Big Woods." I loved it! I was reading about a girl like me that didn't have much, but enjoyed every moment of being a kid.

Since I've grown up, my life has run the gamut from lying awake at night trying to figure out how we were going to pay the bills to the abundance of today. I worked more than three decades to be able to afford enough clothing to outfit a small nation and enough shoes to earn the nickname Imelda Marcos Junior. I have collections to the point of almost having collections of collections.

This brings us to the first of three of Pastor Jim's suggestions, "throw out." I've been doing some of that with bags of clothes and shoes I've taken to Open Door. I know I have to get more serious about paring down on the overload of material possessions.

Pastor Jim hasn't channeled into my internal self; so obviously, I'm not the only one with a crazy busy schedule. My calendar is often double or triple booked. I'm so over stretched that I have reminders of my reminders. "Cut back," he said. Cut back on schedules. If I look through my calendar I can see things I want to do, but those are often pushed aside for something I feel obligated to do. I'm retired but, by golly, that doesn't seem to give me a lot more time. My days are full and often hectic. I haven't found time to write for months and months. Not. One. Story.

Perhaps, part of my time crunch comes from the interruptions of emails, phone calls, social media, Google, and that feeling of constantly being connected. Let's face it…if I forget my phone on a simple trip to town, I'll turn around and get it. My smart phone is like carrying a home office with me everywhere I go. It dings, buzzes, and even whistles at me.

"Turn off," Pastor Jim said. He has a really good point. How do you relax when you are at the beck and call of, well, just about everyone? Not only people you know, but also people you don't know. How the heck did that happen?

By de-cluttering our lives, we have more time to enjoy life's breathtaking moments. We have time to look at a beautiful sunset and admire the way the clouds form in the sky. My brother Donnie and I used to play, "What does that cloud look like?" We saw angels, ships, faces, and all kinds of goofy things in the clouds. Now when I look at a cloud, I might see the possibility of rain, but it's been years since I studied the clouds and tried to picture an object.

I've been under the misguided notion that's the way life is now a days. It doesn't have to be. Is it possible for me to throw out, cut back, and turn off? I've been much too busy chasing the wind to enjoy a mere handful of tranquility.

Alzheimer's Awareness, Go Purple!

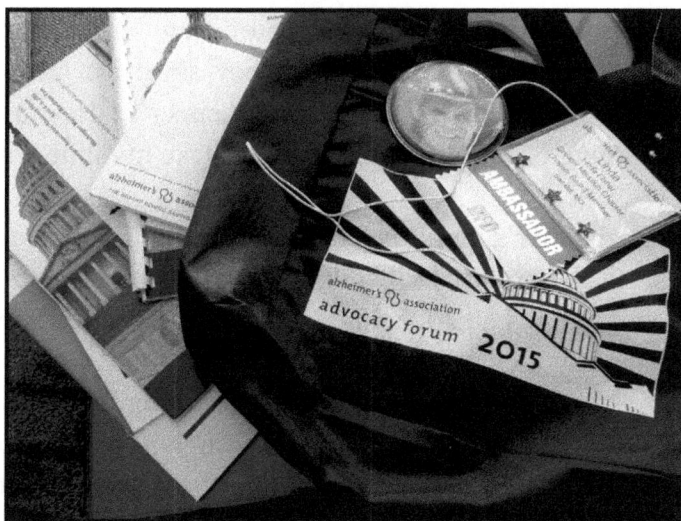

Purple is my favorite color, and coincidentally, it is the Alzheimer's movement color too. June is Alzheimer's and Brain Awareness Month and an ideal time to deck out in purple.

I signed the purple pledge and changed my Facebook profile photo to the "END ALZ" logo. The pledge is to wear purple gear on June 21, the longest day, and throughout the month of June.

The "Longest Day" ties well to Alzheimer's. As any caregiver can attest, some days are not just long—they are endless. Alzheimer's is an equal opportunity disease affecting people like you and me and creeping into the ranks of the famous.

It was interesting to see that the cast of *The Big Bang Theory* have joined the fight against Alzheimer's. Along with other well-known celebrities, they performed at "A Night at Sardi's" to benefit Alzheimer's. They were joined by Joey McIntyre, singer/songwriter and a member of New Kids on the Block. The fight is personal to Joey since his mother recently lost her battle with Alzheimer's. He said, "Mourning is a process, and I have to take my time with it."

Alzheimer's can bring families together, and it can tear them apart. Or both. When Glen Campbell announced he had Alzheimer's, his family was admired for the way they rallied around him. Due to his family's support, Glen was able to perform well after he had the disease. Eventually, he wound up in long-term care. Now the family is at odds with his fourth and present wife, Kim. His children from previous marriages claim Kim Campbell has barred them from seeing their father, failing to provide Glenn with basic personal care items, and being financially irresponsible. Some of his children are trying to get a judge to appoint a guardian to protect his interests.

Often family members disagree on how to provide excellent care for the individual with Alzheimer's. They fuss and fight, and before you know it, they become more focused on having their own way than what is really and truly the best resolution to their quandary.

The more you learn about the disease, the more likely you are to make good decisions. The primary care partner will experience a different level of stress and angst than the occasional visitor. Until you walk in their shoes, be very, very careful about criticizing. This isn't to say that everyone is cut out to be a caregiver.

Some aren't. Unless you are willing and able to step in full-time, proceed with caution. As long as your loved one is not in danger or neglected, be supportive. Be a part of the solution instead of adding to the problems.

Share your stories, your experiences, and show your support for caregivers and people with the disease. Create awareness with the color purple!

My goal is to wear purple every day in June. This is an easy goal for me since I have a wardrobe rich in purple, even without considering all the purple walk shirts I've accumulated over the years. In case I get up and forget to don my Alzheimer's gear, my fingernails and toenails are both polished purple. My toenails have the addition of a layer of sparkle.

Sparkle on the nails makes them look darned cool, but it is a real chore to remove it. That's when I have to drag out the super-duper polish remover pads and sometimes finish with a bottle of remover. If only we could remove Alzheimer's from the face of the earth as if it were a thin layer of polish!

We want to turn the world purple in support of the 47 million people worldwide who are living with dementia. By being an advocate, a supporter, and raising awareness, the brain you save may be your own. GoPurple and #ENDALZ—not just for June, but for a lifetime.

The Most Expensive Disease

Alzheimer's is the most expensive disease in America. Our country faces an impending financial crisis. The cost to Medicare for persons with dementia is three times higher than for seniors without the disease. The emotional impact on caregivers contributes to health issues for them. Caregivers pay an additional $9.7 billion for their own health care.

Dementia is costly to families. It strips away at the family finances. This is a disease fraught with unexpected expenses ranging from adult personal care products to hiring a sitter. Whether caring for a loved one at home or placing them into long-term care, families are hit emotionally and financially on a regular basis. It becomes a way of life.

When facing the dementia financial crisis, families sometimes sell possessions they would have never considered under normal circumstances. Jim and I sold our lake property. It had once been our intention to retire there, but retirement was never to be for us.

Recently, I read an article about ninety-two-year-old Leon Lederman that really made me pause. Lederman, along with two other scientists, received the 1988 Nobel Prize for discovering a subatomic particle. He said it was just collecting dust. His wife mentioned a more practical reason for the sale. They faced financial uncertainty when Lederman was diagnosed with dementia, and the $756,000 they received for the pure gold medal made them more financially secure.

A gold medal doesn't hold the sentimental value of a home. A story that made headlines in May of this year was about a former Japanese prisoner of war who needed around the clock care after being diagnosed with dementia. This story could have taken place in the USA, and probably has. This particular article took place in Cornwall and affected ninety-four-year-old Charles Atkins. His family said the government was "throwing him on the scrapheap." The dilemma for the family was that unless he sold his home, his two daughters were responsible for his expensive care.

Can't happen here, you say? Twenty-eight states have filial responsibility laws where adult children can be forced to provide necessities for their indigent parents, including long-term care. Most states don't enforce these laws, yet. As the crunch becomes tighter for state assistance, they may begin to close their own financial gap. In most states, this involves civil court action, but twelve states impose criminal penalties and three states allow both civil and criminal.

Of course, if you are like me, you want the best care for your parents. Unfortunately, the enormous cost of nursing home care could force middle-class Americans into bankruptcy in a hurry. It's a sticky situation, and if selling the family home gets you and Uncle Sam off the hook, it may seem the lesser evil.

Yes, Alzheimer's is the most expensive disease in America, and it looks like it is only going to become five times more costly by 2050. This puts the exclamation point behind the statement, "End Alzheimer's now!" Without a cure for Alzheimer's, the government and families are going to be faced with the unfaceable, the impossible, the unimaginable.

There is "Hope for Alzheimer's." Science is making great strides toward finding an effective treatment for Alzheimer's and ultimately a cure. We need to keep pestering our legislators! If each of us helps in the fight to end Alzheimer's through awareness, persistence, and downright refusing to give up, we can make a difference. A big, life-changing difference.

What Survivors?

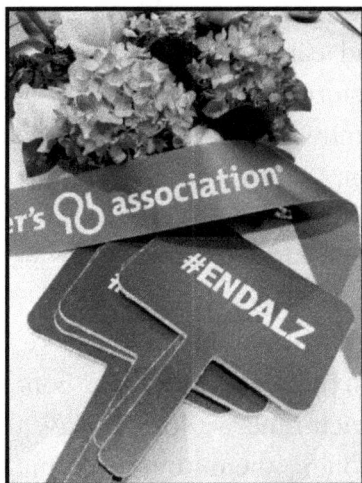

I've been seeing images of a "Limited Edition" T-shirt for Alzheimer's Awareness. The shirt says, "Supporting the Fighters, Admiring the Survivors, Honoring the Taken, And Never Giving Up Hope, Alzheimer's Awareness." People seemed to be excited about buying these T-shirts.

I don't want to burst the bubble of enthusiasm, but this shirt certainly does not promote Alzheimer's awareness. At our annual Walk to End Alzheimer's, we cannot have a victory lap for our survivors. The cold, hard fact is that Alzheimer's leaves no survivors.

Alzheimer's is the sixth leading cause of death in the United States and the only one in the top ten that cannot be prevented, cured, or even slowed. Twenty million Americans understand this harsh reality: five million with the disease and their fifteen million unpaid caregivers.

Alzheimer's *does* have fighters—millions of them. We have warriors with the disease and care partners who raise awareness and dollars so that we can have survivors someday. These brave people share their stories, their struggles, their highs, and lows as they live life to the fullest. They celebrate each moment of joy and refuse to cave in to despair.

Several years ago, I met a forty-year-old woman in Washington, D.C., who had early onset Alzheimer's. As we told our personal stories to our senators and representative, she said, "I know it's too late for me, but I want a cure for my children. I don't want them to have to go through this." She is gone and has been for several years, but we continue her fight to make her wishes come true.

Family members and loved ones honor the taken. Jim was taken before his sixtieth birthday. We honor the loved ones we've lost each time we join a Walk to End Alzheimer's. We honor them by becoming advocates, or "voices," for Alzheimer's research and hounding legislators to push for increased funding.

Advocacy makes a difference! This week we received word that due to the relentless dedication of Alzheimer's advocates, increased research funding is making its way through the legislative process. The House Labor, Health and Human Services Appropriations Subcommittee has approved an additional $300 million in Alzheimer's research.

Harry Johns, Alzheimer's Association CEO said, "Should this increase become law, it will be the largest annual increase ever in federal Alzheimer's research funding. Following today's actions, the full House Appropriations Committee is expected to consider this legislation next week. We also anticipate that the Senate will begin to move their own version of the FY16 Labor-HHS bill next week."

Advocates will never give up hope! The *National Plan to Address Alzheimer's Disease* sets forth a goal to find a cure or effective treatment by 2025. With adequate funding to support the bright scientific minds at work on a cure, our goal is within reach.

When our work is done, I'll be at the front of the line to buy a T-shirt that has "Admire the survivors" on it. Until then, we need to keep the momentum going and stick to the *Plan* to find the elusive cure and/or effective treatment for Alzheimer's *no later* than 2025, but hopefully much, much sooner.

Glen Campbell: I'll Be Me

Last night I watched *Glen Campbell...I'll Be Me* on CNN. The 2014 film documents Glen's Alzheimer's journey.

I heard about the documentary a few years ago at the Alzheimer's Advocacy Forum. My mom went to D.C. with me in 2013 when Glen Campbell was there. He fairly oozed charm and posed to have his photo taken with many of the ladies, including my mom.

I'll Be Me was painful for me to watch. It brought back memories of Jim's loss of communication and musical skills. At least only family witnessed Jim's problems and not a paying audience.

The family told of their struggles to make sure they walked the fine line between the cathartic benefits of Glen performing and being vigilant of him embarrassing himself. Audiences were tolerant. If he played the same song twice, so what? At least they got to see him perform.

Campbell's physician felt that performing on his "Goodbye Tour," doing what Glen loved, helped him maintain the ability to function longer. Sometimes his daughter, Ashley, had to tell her dad the correct key for certain songs. During their "dueling" instruments, her with a banjo, him with his guitar, she admitted that sometimes he didn't always follow along. Glen relied heavily on Teleprompters to remind him of the words to songs he had sung for years.

During his doctor visits, I heard some of the same questions with similar answers during Jim's visits with his neurologist. When asked questions, he couldn't answer, Campbell said, "I don't worry about those things." The doctor asked him who the first president of the United States was and Campbell replied, "My goodness, I don't know. I don't use that very much lately." Jim would typically say, "I have no idea," in a tone that indicated he didn't care to know either.

Ashley testified in front of a congressional hearing on Alzheimer's. Advocates in D.C. for the Alzheimer's Advocacy Forum, wearing purple sashes, packed the room. Ashley's emotional testimony explained the changes in her relationship with her dad. She said it was hard for him to recall her name. Their times fishing together no longer lives in his memories.

When watching old family films, Glen asked, "Who's that?" His wife, Kim, gently supplied the pertinent information: "It's you, honey," or "That's your first wife," or "It's your oldest daughter."

Jim once looked at photos from our honeymoon. I pointed at a photo of me, and playfully said, "Do you know who that is?" His answer, of course, was, "I have no idea." The devil is in the details. Some of the most hurtful moments are when you realize what had been memories shared, become your memories alone.

The film shows the relentless progression of Alzheimer's disease. By the time of his final performance on stage, Glen did not know it was his last performance. Cal Campbell said that when his dad performed, "He actually becomes himself again."

The story ended with the recording session of "I'm Not Going to Miss You." At this point, Glen is already fading away but his eyes sparkle when he finally gets into the song. This song really tugs at the heartstrings. The idea stemmed from Campbell's remark that he couldn't figure out why everyone was so worried about him having Alzheimer's. He said, "It's not like I'm going to miss anyone, anyway."

Kim finally placed Glenn in a home where he could get twenty-four hour care. He is reportedly happy and healthy. He is losing his communication skills and doesn't recognize many of his visitors.

As is often the case, family is feuding. Two of his children by a previous marriage have taken legal action against Kim. This family is torn apart at a time they should be pulling together. Individuals must arrive at acceptance in their own way and on their personal time schedule.

Glen Campbell's Alzheimer's story is heartrending and, oh, so familiar to millions who have lived a similar story.

Anywhere but Here

Serial stowaway, sixty-three-year-old Marilyn Hartman, was caught at O'Hare Airport trying to board a flight without a ticket. While some people are afraid of flying, Marilyn seems to be obsessed with the idea. She's been arrested several times at airports for trying to board without a ticket.

Oddly enough, Ms. Hartman had a valid ticket the day before her arrest, but caused such a disturbance that she was escorted off the plane. I'm beginning to think she wants to be wherever she isn't, including on a plane. She's been arrested on the west coast, Phoenix, and more recently in Chicago—at both O'Hare and Midway. She once remarked to reporters that airports were safer than living on the streets.

Why does she keep trying to stowaway on airplanes when it leads to jail time? She said, "Even smart people do stupid things." Well, that statement is entirely true, but I believe she can't help herself because she wants to be somewhere besides "here," wherever *here* may be.

Maybe all of us have a little of this compulsion to be somewhere else. Who hasn't spent a tough day on the job and had a strong urge to be at a favorite vacation spot instead? This lady carried it to an entirely different level.

When we're young, we long to grow up. Once we are grownups, we want the carefree days of our youth. Time and space can be our friend or our enemy.

People with Alzheimer's often want to be in a different place. They pace. They want to go home, even though they are at home. They want to be somewhere else. Anywhere but where they are.

Wandering is a common problem with Alzheimer's. It's dangerous for the person and worrisome for the family. Think about how confusing and strange their world is, and it's easier to understand why they want to find what they've lost. Their shattered memory may tell them they live in a certain house, even though they once knew that it had been sold or torn down.

I knew a man with Alzheimer's who wandered off frequently and walked across town to the house where once he had lived with his first wife. She still lived there, and when he showed up, she phoned his current wife to come and get him. She would offer him coffee, or breakfast, while they waited.

When life gets tough, we often want to place distance between where we actually are and where we theoretically could be. It's fight or flight. While most of us fight, a few of us flee.

Maybe Ms. Hartman really is smart and finds jail to be safer than the streets. It probably doesn't hurt to have three guaranteed meals a day. I believe she knows her chances of boarding without a "ticket to ride" are slim. I would say slim to none, but she managed to fly from San Jose to Los Angeles without a ticket.

Some people try to run away from their problems. Could Ms. Hartman be trying to run away from herself? When she is released from jail, we'll be hearing about her again. And again. A serial stowaway headed for nowhere or anywhere but where she is.

New Treatments for Brain Diseases

Alzheimer's is a global problem and scientists from around the world share information in a unified effort to find an effective treatment or cure for Alzheimer's disease. Representing sixty-five countries, more than 4,000 scientists gathered in Washington, D.C., for the Alzheimer's Association International Conference 2015.

One of the exciting developments of this year's conference is a report that new drugs have yielded promising early results for treatment of several brain diseases. Finding the key to effectively treating Alzheimer's disease may unlock the mystery of other neurodegenerative diseases. Scientists have found common components of several brain diseases, including Alzheimer's, Parkinson's, and Lewy body dementia.

What do these diseases have in common? They all cause brain cell death because of a change in the shape of a protein. This protein can become toxic and affects the nerve cells or synapses. The proteins that affect Alzheimer's disease are beta-amyloid and tau. Lewy bodies are the protein associated with Parkinson's and Lewy body dementia. Misfolded proteins bind to other proteins and form large aggregates.

What are some of the drugs being tested? Richard Fisher, PhD, NeuroPhage Pharmaceuticals, Cambridge, MA, and a group of colleagues are researching NPT088. This drug has been tested on animal models with Parkinson's and Alzheimer's. In most cases, it reduced levels of amyloid beta, tau, and alpha-synuclein (the main component of Lewy bodies). Animal models showed improved memory. Clinical trials should take place in 2016.

Another new drug, TRV101, is being tested in Toronto, ON, Canada, by Treventis Corporation. This group used computer models to screen more than 11 million compounds to find ones that could prevent toxic proteins. In test tubes, TRV 101 is capable of allowing natural clearing mechanisms to remove protein aggregates. Clearing toxic proteins should improve cognitive function. This research has moved to animal testing.

Alzheimer's is a complicated disease and a cure has been elusive. Effective treatment is more likely to be a cocktail of drugs, rather than a single medication. This is similar to how HIV/AIDs and other disorders are treated.

As with other major diseases, lifestyle changes are part of the treatment for Alzheimer's. Researchers are optimistic that Alzheimer's risk has declined for recent generations due to better cardiovascular care, blood pressure management, controlling diabetes, and realizing the importance of physical activity and a healthy diet.

The great thing about lifestyle changes, you don't have to wait for a drug to come down the pipeline, you can just jump in and begin! Right now improving a healthy diet is an easy fix with fresh vegetables from my garden. This is one time of the year that something that tastes good, homegrown tomatoes, is good for me.

People today are more socially active. At least I know I am. Reading the news on my smart phone or having articles delivered to my in-box keeps my mind active. For fun, I throw in a few crossword puzzles or read a book.

Between research and common sense practices, we are moving in the right direction to make Alzheimer's a distant memory.

Once in a Blue Moon

There's been a lot of talk about blue moons lately.

"Why is the moon going to turn blue?" my granddaughter asked a few weeks ago when we were talking about the upcoming blue moon. Her mom explained that a "blue" moon had nothing to do with color and meant two full moons occur in one month.

We recently had a blue moon—at least according to some sources, but in our time of too much information, some purists disagree with this definition. Up until 1946, a blue moon was the third full moon in an astronomical season with four full moons. The confusion came about when James Pruett, a hobby astronomer, published an article that said a second full moon in one month was a blue moon. Although the mistake was noted and refuted, the information had already spread worldwide and became the accepted definition of a blue moon.

Let's face it. It's much easier to notice a second moon in one month than to determine how many full moons occur in a season. According to the original definition of a blue moon, the one we just celebrated was not, in fact, a blue moon. One that we will ignore, most likely, will occur May 21, 2016,—the third full moon in an astronomical season. But we will easily notice the one January 31, 2018, the second full moon in the month.

By either definition, a blue moon doesn't occur too often, and the expression, "once in a blue moon" means something that happens rarely. Some reasons for those "once in a blue moon" occurrences:

1. Something we don't like to do and put off. In this category are chores like washing windows, cleaning the garage, and pulling weeds. Tedious, time-consuming tasks that always seem better left for another day. The same goes for uncomfortable, routine medical tests like mammograms, colonoscopies, or endoscopies. Procrastination, indeed!

2. We've gotten out of the habit. We haven't gone to church for a while, so Sunday seems like the perfect day to sleep late. After missing two or three club or committee meetings, we are out of the loop, and choose to leave it that way.

3. Not enough time. Life is so busy now that we don't have time to phone a friend much less visit a loved one with Alzheimer's in the nursing home. Busy, busy, busy. That's how most of us live now. We're so busy being busy that we miss out on the important things in life.

Maybe in reality, it is fine for some things to happen once in a blue moon, but others shouldn't. It's really up to each of us to decide what goes into which category—once in a blue moon or much more frequently. Just living isn't nearly as important as having a life.

In my world, things that happen once in a blue moon, or rarely, could be considered somewhat common. I'm okay with that most of the time, but sometimes I have regrets that I didn't make that phone call or visit a loved one. Maybe, at least once in a blue moon, I should take time to lounge in a lawn chair in the shade of the oak tree, sip a mint julep, and read a trashy novel.

Walk the Walk, Talk the Talk

Jessica Snell, Sedalia Walk to End Alzheimer's co-chair, and I were at the radio station Tuesday morning to talk about the Walk to End Alzheimer's. We were armed with the names of our sponsors and teams, goals, and statistics. It's always a pleasure to be on the air with Doug, and even better to record the program for broadcast the next day. When you are on the air live, you just have to go with it, but when the program is recorded and your tongue gets tangled, you get "overs." We all need overs from time to time.

I've been involved with the walk since 1998 and during that time, I've seen numerous changes. The first year, I raise $400 and Jim and I walked with a handful of people. For the next five years, I was the coordinator, or walk chair, of our local Memory Walk. At that time, our logo was the word "Alzheimer's" with the "H" being two people, leaning. The Alzheimer's Association was well known as "Someone to lean on." The walk began to draw hundreds of walkers.

For the next five years, Shelley Spinner coordinated our walk, and I backed off the committee to make sure everyone saw her as the leader of the group. She did a great job of keeping the walk exciting and fresh. I was able to concentrate on being captain of Jim's Team.

Following Shelley, Lisa Hayworth led the walk committee for two years. Lisa had no experience or help. At that time, my sister-in-law Ginger and I went back on the committee, and we've remained on it since then helping Sheila Ream.

Some things change and others remain the same. The Alzheimer's Association changed the logo to the current one and "Memory Walk" to Walk to End Alzheimer's. Some of the format has changed. The Promise Garden ceremony has been added and it encompasses the different ways that Alzheimer's affects us. Our local chapter has changed names from Mid-Missouri to Greater Missouri, merged with the Southwest Chapter, and became a national chapter. What does this all mean? We still have chapter offices where they were located previously and the Alzheimer's Association still provides the personal service that helped me throughout the years when dementia ruled our lives.

Another change I've seen over the years is how people have become more knowledgeable about the disease. When I first approached area businesses in 1999 for corporate sponsorship, no one seemed to know much about Alzheimer's. Now, everyone seems to know a few basics. A lot of credit goes to the Alzheimer's Association for raising public awareness.

The walk is about people. It is a time to show care and concern for those with the disease and their loved ones. It is a time when everyone puts aside their differences and embraces the opportunity to support their friends, neighbors, and relatives who are dealing with Alzheimer's. We have teams with different names, but in essence, we are all one team. Competition is fierce, but friendly. I celebrate the teams that raise more than our team.

When I was coordinating the Sedalia walk, I became friends with Ted Distler who coordinated the Jefferson City walk. We "trash talked" each other all the time about which town was going to raise more money. In truth, it was all in competitive fun, and we supported each other at fundraisers. Ted would drive to Sedalia for our Dance to Remember, and I'd drive to Jefferson City for their Chicken Dinner. We had the same connection to the disease and the same passion for doing what we could to help other care partners and persons with dementia.

What people don't understand is Walk to End Alzheimer's is a fun event. Yes, it is sobering at times when you hear the stories of the participants, and the flower ceremony is touching, but knowing that you are doing your part is heart lifting. Smiles, laughter, and love are the order of the day. You don't want to miss it or you'll have to wait another year. From babies in strollers to seniors in wheelchairs, we lend support and lean on each other to end Alzheimer's.

Like a Bridge over Troubled Waters

Rob popped in another video to dub. Christmas, 1991. Jim and his brother Billy began to sing "Bridge over Troubled Waters" in their close harmony. My heart stopped to hear his voice, see him on the somewhat grainy film—standing straight, playing his classic Fender guitar.

Watching our home videos made me laugh and made me cry. Jim narrated as he filmed everything around him for "posterity." No event was too small or insignificant. He chose the family member he was making the video for and encouraged everyone to say "hi" to that person. One tape was for his brother Bob, "and Barbara, too," he added when he remembered he hadn't mentioned her. A Thanksgiving tape at my mom's house was specifically for my brother Jimmy who was in the Navy in California.

"Did Dad ever send these videos to the people he made them for?" Rob asked me.

"No. That's why we still have them," I said. One time after he became confused, Jim made an audiotape for his cousin Leroy. His mom saw him walk out to the mailbox and raise the flag. Curious, she went out to see what he was mailing. Inside the mailbox was a cassette tape with "for Leroy" written on it. No postage. No wrapping. No address.

Jim's personality and humor uplifted the videos to an experience. Most of Jim's family loved the camera. His uncles and cousins would ham it up in standup comedian mode. Uncle Jewel described his many personalities and mashed his face flat in one video. Jim interviewed his cousin Buddy about the lady ranger bawling him out over not coming to a complete stop at the campground's exit. "Don't they have stop signs in Missouri?" Jim asked.

The highlights of the old home videos are family gatherings. Houses and yards overflowed with family. Guitars, fiddles, microphones, and amplifiers were dragged out for impromptu family concerts. Everyone had their "special" songs to sing and requests rang out from the audience for their favorites.

I loved being able to see and hear Jim tell his corny jokes, tall tales, but most of all, I loved to hear him sing. I watched the tapes of him singing through blurred eyes. He and his brother Billy sang several songs, and the song "Bridge over Troubled Waters" was almost prophetic. It told a story of comfort, friends, dreams, and having that person to hold you up when times are rough. More important it told the kind of man Jim was. He was always on my side. He was my husband, my friend, my bridge. He encouraged me to shine.

In addition to stealing Jim's musical talent, dementia stole his voice. It seems like a small miracle to hear his voice after all the years of silence. When the darkness of dementia fell, he was no longer able to dry my tears or be my bridge. I had to find my own way back into the light.

It was almost twenty years ago when we learned the hard truth of dementia. We made the most of the time we had until the journey ended April 18, 2005, when Jim was fifty-nine years old. Thursday, August 27, would have been Jim's seventieth birthday. It would have been a day of celebration, but now it is a time of remembrance. And gratitude for the adventures we shared.

Jim is gone from our world, but his essence lives on the videotapes and in his children and grandchildren. Last week when Whitney pulled out her ukulele, her mother said, "Your Grandpa Jim could have taught you so much." Just like her grandpa, she is collecting different instruments to play. When I see Whitney's short videos online, it makes me think that her Grandpa Jim would have been capturing every moment he could for "posterity."

Music and family were the great loves of Jim's life. We are fortunate to have those magical memories stored in our hearts and on the old videotapes.

Just like the Good Old Days

A couple of days ago, Harold popped a big bowl of popcorn and we settled in front of the TV to watch the old episodes of *Castle* recorded on our DVR. I pushed the "on" button, and nothing happened. After pushing on/off/select numerous times, the most I could get on the TV was "no signal."

Harold tried to reset the satellite receiver without success, so it was time to call DISH. After a half hour of trying this, selecting that, and retrying to acquire a signal, a heavily accented voice said they would be mailing us a new receiver.

After some tough negotiations, Harold convinced them they needed to send a repairperson to come out and set up the new receiver. They will be here Tuesday. So without any other kind of reception, we are without a TV.

Being without a TV isn't so bad. It reminded me of the good old days when we didn't watch TV in the summer because all programs were reruns. So what did we do without all the extensive programming on TV? Well, we read books and spent time outside. Thank goodness, I had a book on my Kindle to read, and I had gone a little overboard at Books-A-Million when I was in Branson.

The spending time outside has worked well. Friday, I spent the day with my mom and sister. We visited, and ate at Country Kitchen. I didn't miss TV at all. The real acid test was Saturday. As it turned out, my major complaint with Saturday was that there wasn't enough time to take a break. We were up early and fixed a big breakfast—different from our routine of coffee and bagel in front of the TV. After a day of mowing, yard work, and going to town, the day was over, and I hadn't gotten a single thing marked off my personal task list. Determined to get at least one thing checked off, I worked until nearly midnight. TV? What's that?

This morning, I dragged myself out of bed for early church services. I wore one of my purple Alzheimer's shirts and picked up a copy of *Broken Road: Navigating the Alzheimer's Labyrinth* to give to Pastor Jim for being the inspiration for some of my blog posts.

As I walked into the sanctuary, they had me choose a rock. "You'll need it during the service," was the explanation. I was hopeful we weren't going to "stone" anyone for his or her transgressions.

I go to contemporary services at the Celebration Center. We have a band and the lyrics to our songs are displayed on a screen. One of our pastors, Nick, brought a message about the traditional Methodist Hymnal and the "rules" for singing the songs. The rules included learning the tunes, singing them exactly as they are written, everyone should sing (take up your cross and bear it, if necessary), sing lustfully (not as half-dead or asleep), yet modestly without destroying the harmony, keep time and sing with the leading voices, and most of all sing spiritually.

Hymnals have the traditional hymns that we sang back in the "good old days." After the message from First Samuel about a stone he called Ebenezer, we sang a traditional hymn, "Come, Thou Fount of Every

Blessing." The women sang the melody and the men repeated a line. It was really quite beautiful, and I think John Wesley would have been proud.

One of the lines in the song is, "Here I raise my Ebenezer." As we sang the song, we came forward in the same manner as communion and placed our rocks on the altar. It was a touching moment that made me feel like I'd taken a step back to another, simpler time.

Maybe the "good old days" weren't always good, but something about them tugs at the heart. It's the place of our memories and the roots of our traditions. Those were days when we were young and full of hope.

Taking a step back for a few days is a welcome relief. Soon, very soon, I'll be ready to return to watching my favorite programs, but for now—I'm doing just fine without TV.

Don't Let the Rain Dampen Your Spirits

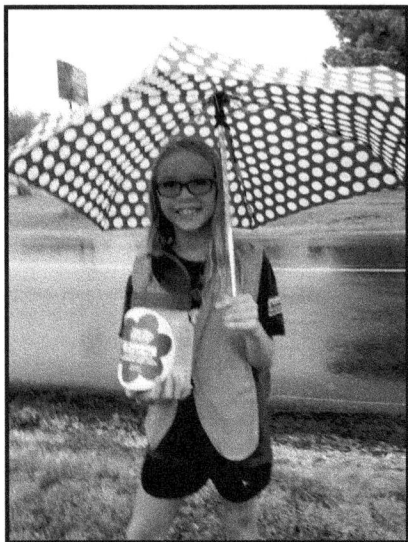

In "The Rainy Day" Henry Wadsworth Longfellow said, "Into each life some rain must fall." At times, we pray for rain, the refreshing life-essential drops that come from the heavens to end droughts. Other times, when we have an important outdoor activity we don't want it to rain. We wonder why it can't hold off for a while longer. Is that too much to ask?

Labor Day is our day for our big Walk to End Alzheimer's fundraiser for Jim's team. This was our 17th year to do the "traffic stop." It seems the day is usually unbearably hot, and this year looked to be more of the same. Then, the forecast called for heat and a chance of rain.

"Will you still do the stop if it rains, or will you reschedule," my niece asked the day before.

"We can't reschedule it. If it rains, we'll stand in the rain. If we have a thunderstorm, we'll wait it out in our cars," I said. In all the previous years, we only had one rainy day. It was a blessing in disguise because the intermittent, gentle showers made for a cooler day.

As we began setting up our signs, a few gentle drops fell. Not bad, I thought. Suppose to last only a short while and move out. Soon, the rain began falling a little harder, and eventually, those of us who brought umbrellas stood beneath them. Only Shelly and Chris didn't have umbrellas. Chris was wearing a raincoat, but Shelly stood alongside the road with her collection can without protection against the rain that stalled over our heads.

I glanced down the street and saw a woman coming out of her house carrying a smiley-face umbrella. She talked to Shelly for a few minutes and handed her the umbrella. This woman had lived in the house for eleven years and noticed us every year. She told Shelly that she admired our tenacity to continue through the hot days in the past. She gave Shelly a donation and insisted she take the umbrella. The woman told Shelly that her sister was only in her fifties and had been diagnosed with early-onset Alzheimer's.

The relentless rain fell on our "parade" until the last half hour. Water was running down the ditches, and the umbrellas didn't keep the rain from soaking us. I didn't mind the wet shirt and Capri's nearly as much as sloshing around with wet socks and shoes. Hey, it was still better than one-hundred degree heat. We didn't let the rain dampen our spirits.

In his poem, Longfellow isn't speaking of physical rain. He is speaking of the dark times when we cling to the past and "days are dark and dreary." It makes me think of a conversation I had with a caregiver recently. She was battling depression and felt overwhelmed taking care of her husband who has Alzheimer's. Yet, while we talked, I could tell she had the courage and indomitable spirit to keep on keeping on.

We all deal with our own personal rainy days. Sometimes they are gentle showers, and we can shrug them off. We can even soldier through those steady downpours without much ado. Then there are those times when the wind is gusting, the thunder is booming, and a torrential downpour flash floods all over our last ray of optimism.

Before you let rainy, turbulent times dampen your spirits, remember the sun is still above those pesky clouds. Sunshine after a rain is glorious; rays beam down like the word of God, and the rainbow promises better days to come.

On the Inside

Our Walk to End Alzheimer's was Saturday. Nearly a full year of preparation all came together for a flawless event. The one thing you can't really control is the weather, but it cooperated in a big way. The day was gorgeous, and for once, I didn't have butterflies worrying about whether it was going to rain…or be so hot that someone could have heatstroke.

Before the walk, we determined the eldest walker, Uncle Johnny, and the youngest, Bella Howard, a sweet baby wearing a Fair View shirt. The best individual fundraiser, Jessica Snell, was announced. Trophies were awarded to Sylvia G. Thompson Residence Center for best fundraising and largest team.

Jessie from the Greater Missouri Chapter surprised me with an award. She pulled out a photo collage that immediately brought back memories. She asked me to say a few words.

"They caught me off guard," I said. Then, I became so choked up, I had to pause before I could continue. Normally, when I speak, I prepare myself mentally to keep the emotions on the inside. After a brief pause, I was able to thank the wonderful walkers and teams that have supported our efforts throughout the years. Then, I told everyone how important the walk was to me personally and how it helped me through the tough times. It gave me a focus and a way to feel good about helping put an end to this awful disease.

The extra bonus for the day was that the weather was also perfect for the other two outdoor events I planned to attend. At three o'clock, my great-niece was married in the same locale where we held the walk—the Highway Gardens on the Fairgrounds.

The final event to end my day was to watch "Changed By Grace" perform at the Sedalia Rockin' for Jesus show. Besides the spiritual implications of the evening, two of the band members happen to be my nephews Mike Munsterman and Larry Cooper.

I thoroughly enjoyed their uplifting performance and their testimonies. A song that really made me think about life was one Larry wrote, "On the Inside." The song is about how we work to have all the material possessions, but then fall into the trap of devoting our lives to gaining even more worldly goods. Looking successful on the outside does not necessarily make a person happy or feel good about how he got to that point in his life. In the song, Larry shares the importance of living life in such a way that a person feels good on the inside.

Mike, too, has found a way to feel good on the inside. Mike has put his life back together after losing his wife Krystal.  He has made a positive impact on the homeless through Krystal's Dream. He has traveled far and wide to provide shoes and socks to those who have fallen on hard times. Through his mission, he has taken a tragedy that could have broken him, and turned it into action to help others.

To feel good on the inside you have to find that sweet spot in your soul where love, peace, and spirituality come to life. The important times in our lives are the heart moments spent doing what we love and being with those we love.

Does it get any better than living life in such a manner that it really does make us feel good on the inside? Sometimes, we should put aside the negative thoughts and pressures that daily life brings and focus on the positive, happy times that make us smile.

Family Matters

On a cold February night, as we were getting ready for bed, I casually mentioned to Harold that this was my year to host our family get-together. We used to gather on Thanksgiving at my mom and dad's house. After Dad died, and Mom sold the house to my brother Mitchell, we converged on them for several years until we made a change with tradition. We decided to pass the hosting around by going from oldest to youngest and decided to meet in September when the weather was better.

"When were you going to tell me this?" he asked.

"Oh, about August," I replied. Harold is the planner. I, on the other hand, am a seat-of-the-pants type person.

Well, he wasn't having any of that. After a barrage of questions about logistics, I finally suggested we have the event at the park so we wouldn't have to find tables, chairs, etc., that he was worrying about seven months ahead of time.

By March, we had rented the shelter at the park and worked on a list of things to do. In addition to the place, the host family provides the meat, drinks, and table service.

The reunion was Sunday, and we couldn't have asked for better weather. We were up at 6:00 a.m. and Harold was in drill-sergeant mode. Before I could get a cup of coffee, he was slicing up the pork loin we'd cooked the day before, and one of the huge hams he had bought for the occasion.

By the time we got the first ham in the roaster oven, it was full. Harold was still fretting that we weren't going to have enough meat. "That's plenty," I said. After all, Stacey was bringing two turkey breasts.

"This isn't like the Fisher reunion," I said. The Fisher reunion is for anyone with the last name, but this reunion is for our immediate family, children, grandchildren, and great-grandchildren. "We usually have about thirty people, not a hundred."

He finally settled on cooking an additional three-pound ham, just in case. Then we fixed gallons and gallons of tea. Thank goodness, Rob came by with his pickup to help us load everything into his truck and our Tahoe.

On the way to town, I began to feel the excitement. Until then, I'd been too busy. I love spending time with my family, and don't see them as often as I should.

Both my sons were there and my two youngest grandchildren. My two oldest grandkids work on weekends, but Whitney would be coming by on her lunch hour. Rob set up a PC to play a CD made from a video of a Capps family Thanksgiving from the early 1990s. Mom was taking a turkey out of the oven, and my husband Jim was running the video camera.

After everyone found the right shelter, we decided to go ahead and start eating. My brother Mitchell had not arrived, but he called to say he was on his way. Tommy asked a short blessing. "Wow, that must be the shortest blessing you've ever done," I said.

"He's still going on the videotape," someone said. Sure enough, the CD was still rolling and Tommy was still asking the blessing. In all fairness, we used to update everyone on our family, and he had the largest family.

We visited and took photos of the brothers, sisters, and our mom. Marshall wasn't able to come this year and our brother Donnie passed away Thanksgiving eve in 2012.

The time flew by, and before it seemed possible, people were leaving. It had been a beautiful day to spend with people I love. Of all things in life, family matters the most.

So You Had a Bad Day

Last week during the full-blood-super-moon eclipse, I discovered that I wasn't my normal self. I woke up at 10:30 a.m. after an extraordinarily long night of nightmare-infested slumber. To say I got up on the wrong side of the bed is an understatement—it was more like I got up on the wrong side of the house. Cranky, headachy, and on the verge of tears, it's no wonder my husband retreated to his office for the day. His main was to steer clear of the crazy woman in the kitchen.

There was no explanation for the way I felt. It just was, and it wasn't going away. It all boiled down to simply having a bad day.

What causes us to have a bad day? Most of the time, it is because of external problems beyond our control that make us nervous or unhappy. Too often, we let the behavior of others ruin an otherwise good day. Someone makes a hurtful or disparaging remark that sinks its ugly roots into our self-esteem and the worry of its validity gnaws at our self-worth. Some bad days, like the one I had, are internal. An unsettling night had spilled over into the daylight.

Anyone can have a bad day, but people with dementia have more than their share. When you take into account their daily wrestling match with confusion and the other symptoms Alzheimer's causes, it helps you understand how bad days can be plentiful.

The unfortunate nature of a bad day is that it can be contagious. When the person with dementia has a bad day, the caregiver has a bad day too.

So what the heck can you do about that? It's hard enough to deal with yourself, much less someone else, when emotions are out of whack, common sense is on vacation, and patience abandoned ship.

It's time to give yourself a time-out. Do something you really love to do, even if you can spare only a few minutes. Some suggestions: a half-hour comedy (I can't possibly stay depressed watching the *Golden Girls*), read a magazine or a chapter in a good book, go for a walk, call your mom or a good friend, or bake cookies.

After your time-out, take a few deep breaths, and if you baked cookies, now would be a good time to have some with a glass of milk. Now, you are ready to stay calm—the number one method for handling your loved one's bad day. Hopefully, you've regained your ability to be patient, because you will need an abundance of it.

A good rule to remember is that what worked yesterday may not work today, so be flexible. Distraction is your friend. If your loved one is crying, or in a really bad mood, you may want to scoop up an ice cream cone. One thing that always worked with Jim was taking a drive. He loved getting in the car and heading down the road. An even better trip for him was when we stopped by DQ for a milkshake.

When a person with dementia has a bad day, it shows in his behavior. Though easier said than done, your best response is to address the emotion rather than the behavior.

There is no one cause for a bad day and there isn't one solution. I think my bad day was the result of a bad night and, of course, the full moon. Probably the real reason is that I'm human with human emotions. So, I had a bad day. It wasn't the first, and rest assured, it won't be the last.

October Fun: Ghost Tour

My grandkids always want me to tell them spooky stories. I have several to choose from about my younger days when Jim and I managed to live in some scary places and had strange experiences galore.

It only stood to reason that when my mom, sisters, and I planned a girls' mini-vacation at Hannibal, a ghost tour would be on the agenda. In all my extensive travels, I had never visited the town that served as Mark Twain's inspiration for *Tom Sawyer*.

We arrived in Hannibal at a good time to take a trolley tour to get the lay of the land. While we were waiting, a "Ghost Tour" sign caught our attention. We strolled inside and signed up for a tour at 7:00 p.m.

During the day, we rode the riverboat and still squeezed in a little shopping. My sisters and I bought vintage hats to wear on the ghost tour.

Our ghost tour guides, Ken and Lisa, asked whether we were more interested in history or ghosts. Our preference was both, so we heard about Hannibal's rich history and haunted tales. During the tour, we stopped in front of several bed and breakfasts, an old church, and the Rockcliffe Mansion. Ken and Lisa had lived in the mansion and told us chilling stories of their adventures. Doors slamming and footsteps on the stairs would be enough to make me hide my head beneath the covers.

The mansion's history is unusual. In its time, it was the biggest and most opulent mansion in Missouri. Lumber baron John J. Cruikshank chose a spot already occupied by a mansion. He moved the offending house next door and eventually his daughter lived there. After Cruikshank died, his widow moved from Rockcliffe to her daughter's home leaving nearly all her belongings behind.

Rockcliffe remained abandoned for forty-three years, its windows broken out, and the rite-of-passage for teenagers was to go into the house to the third floor and rip off a piece of the map in the children's room. I'm sure it was considered a sign of bravery to accomplish this route without freaking out. Although, the mansion's ghosts are considered to be friendly, Casper-type ghosts, I decided that I wouldn't want to spend the night there.

Our tour ended with a trip to the cemetery, spooky to be sure. Although I'd visited a cemetery on a previous ghost tour, it was not like this one. The other cemetery was in the middle of Boston and well lighted. This cemetery was on the edge of town, no lights, and although it had been cleaned up, it was still an old, old cemetery with toppled stones around the fringes. We were furnished with divining rods and tiny two-inch flashlights. I wouldn't touch the rods after we were instructed how to get yes and no answers, because it reminded me of a Ouija board pointer. I've had some hair-raising experiences with Ouija boards, and I didn't want to call up any spirits without Ghost Busters on speed dial.

The next day, after visiting the museum and Twain's boyhood home, we toured Rockcliffe. You've heard about pictures that have eyes that follow you no matter where you are. Well, there's a photo of John Cruikshank that does. I'm not ashamed to say that's a little bit creepy. After seeing the bedrooms, I'm sure I would not have had a restful night had we chosen to stay there. Old clothes, hats, and shoes in the closet made me think the lady of the manor might return to change her clothing.

To finish our journey, we drove into Illinois looking for Burbridge Cemetery where several of our ancestors are buried. We got lost. We finally asked a local and he directed us to it. My sister consulted her genealogy book and we found several graves listed in the book. We took photos and headed for home.

It is always fun to spend time with family. It's something most of us put aside for the busy, mundane things we do in life. Sometimes, it helps to take a step back and think about how after we're gone a stone may be the only visible reminder of our time on earth. Someday, that stone may be part of a ghost tour and a tourist with a divining rod may be asking us yes and no questions. Wouldn't it be so much fun to groan loudly and say, "Get your big fat foot off my head!"

One Big Fat Fib We All Tell

I was at Walmart yesterday and the woman checking my groceries asked, "How are you?"

"Fine," I answered. "And how are you?"

Thank goodness, neither of us answered the question with great thought as to how things were really going. What if she had launched into a story about her husband's cousin's wife's surgery with complete gory details while the person in line behind me tried to run over me with his cart?

About 99.9 percent of the time, if I ask how someone is, he replies, "Fine." I noticed that Jim retained this "polite" conversational tool when his dementia was so advanced he could barely speak. If someone said, "How are you?" he would answer, "Fine." He wasn't able to verbalize just how awful his diagnosis was even if he'd wanted to share his state of being.

During the dark days when I was his caregiver, I never once answered a stranger's polite inquiry with the truth. It was always the stock, and expected, answer.

Occasionally, you will get a more personal question, "How are you holding up?" from someone who knows the circumstances of your life. In that case, you might answer something like, "Things have been better." Even with that hint of a problem, you will most likely go on your un-merry way to avoid sharing your problems.

I recently saw a Wisdom Quote on Facebook that said, "The worst part about being strong is that no one ever asks if you're okay." It is true that when someone is caring for a loved one with a serious illness, often people only ask about the person with the health problem. They don't stop to consider that often the caregiver is exhausted physically and drained emotionally.

Most of us don't like to be whiners. Plain and simple. Yet, there are those among us who love to whine. I do know certain people that I've learned the hard way to avoid the simple "How are you" question. These are the people who suffer the woe-is-me attitude if they have a hangnail. They will go on and on and on and on…then, when they have to "run" they throw off a casual "How are you" and walk away without waiting for an answer.

Even honest people tell this little white lie. I guess if you're having a really bad day, it's better than bursting into tears in the middle of the grocery store. No one wants to have a complete meltdown in public. Well, *almost* no one. Once again, there are those who try to get sympathy, or maybe a handout, from strangers.

It isn't easy to avoid the pleasantries either. One day at a checkout, the young woman asked, "How are you?" I replied "Fine" as I tried to get the card to swipe. "I'm fine too," she said. "Thanks for asking." It sounded a whole lot like a rebuke to me for not continuing a pointless exchange. Or did she simply hear what she expected?

I plan to continue with social pleasantries, even when it's a big fat fib—at least with strangers. With whiners, I might say "hello" and avoid eye contact.

Once in a Lifetime

On Sunday, I was working at the Sedalia Business Women's Chicken Dinner when I saw an elderly lady sitting all alone at a table. Unlike everyone else, she did not have a plate of chicken and trimmings in front of her.

She had a lost look, and instinctively I knew she had dementia. Concerned that she had wandered in and didn't have a ticket, I walked over to her and asked, "Are you hungry for chicken?" I had already decided that if she didn't have a ticket, I'd buy her lunch.

She smiled at me, tilted her hand back and forth, and murmured some indiscernible words. I smiled at her and walked to the ticket table.

"Do you know who that lady is?" I asked.

"No, but I think she has Alzheimer's. Her husband is fixing her plate."

I milled around, refilling drinks, cleaning trays and tables. Eventually, a woman walked up to me, read my nametag and asked, "Are you the Linda Fisher I saw in the paper that's involved with the Alzheimer's Association." I told her I was. With tears in her eyes, she told me her husband had Alzheimer's, and that she had always wanted to meet me.

Later, another woman introduced herself to me to let me know a mutual friend had steered her toward my blog. Her husband, only in his sixties, had Alzheimer's.

Eventually, I worked my way back to the table where the lady sat with her husband eating her chicken dinner. She spotted me and reached out to give me a hug. "I love you," she said as she kissed me on the cheek. I hugged her back. When the hug ended, she kissed my hand.

Her husband smiled and said, "She thinks everyone is the Pope."

I introduced myself and told him my husband had passed away at fifty-nine from dementia.

"Then, you understand what we are going through," he said.

"Yes, I do," I said. We chatted for a while about caregivers. He had just hired a new one. He was dismayed with the lack of help and support he had found. He told me he didn't have a computer, I took his name and phone number to pass on to the Alzheimer's Association.

It doesn't matter where we are or what we are doing, the chances are good we will run into someone who has a personal connection with Alzheimer's— people filled with questions and looking for answers. Caregivers muddle through the disease doing the best they can based on trial and error.

Unfortunately, when I look into the face of someone with Alzheimer's or the faces of caregivers, I don't have all the answers to their questions. All I can really do is offer hugs or hug back when I'm being hugged. Offer support and caring. Listen. Accept human flaws. Know that the worst response is indifference.

I'm thankful that these people shared their personal stories, and thankful for the opportunity to share a hug with a lovely woman who happens to have Alzheimer's. I'm grateful for a glimpse into her life—learn she was once a teacher, know she has a life beyond the scope of the disease, and grateful she has a husband who fixes her plate and looks out for her well-being.

Alzheimer's disease is as unpredictable as life itself. Each day is a new adventure and a new experience. Yesterday, I met a charming lady named Alice, and just like in Lisa Genova's book, she is *still* Alice. Thanks to her, a chicken dinner turned into a once in a lifetime experience of being mistaken for the Pope, and to share a few unforgettable moments with a loving, good-hearted woman named Alice.

Turn Back Time

Today we turned our clocks back one hour. My cell phone and computer both did it for me, but the dozen or so other clocks remain an hour ahead until they are changed.

I always remember which way to turn the clocks by "spring forward" for daylight saving time and "fall back" to return to standard time. In one place, I saw it referred to as "turn back time."

Turning back time is completely appropriate for another reason than standard time on November 1. This is the day after Halloween and the religious holiday of "All Saints Day" or as it is celebrated in some countries, "Day of the Dead."

Is there any better way to turn back time than to remember those who have already passed away? It's strange that I've never thought of this day as the Day of the Dead and never knew much about that tradition. On this day, millions of people will make annual pilgrimages to cemeteries and churches. Graves will be decorated with offerings of sugar skulls, flowers, or favorite food and beverage. Prayers are offered for the spiritual passing of loved ones.

Although I never celebrated the Day of the Dead, for some reason the past week has been an extreme time of reflection for me. On the hour-long drive to my Alzheimer's board meeting, I reminisced during the drive over and, again, on the way back.

Who would think something as simple as rolling dips in the road could bring back a vivid memory? Jim used to hit those dips fast enough that my stomach would feel funny. I drove past the house on Newland hill where we lived when our kids were little. I thought about them standing at the end of the driveway waiting for the school bus. I remembered Christmas, Halloween, and sitting around the dinner table. I remembered bits and pieces of the life we once had— before time marched on.

I passed the turnoff to Arrow Rock and thought of the good times we spent there. Remembered the time Jim wandered off during the festival and it took my sister, her husband, and me some scary moments before we found him.

Even before I drove past the cancer hospital, the drive alone made me think of taking my co-worker and friend, Diane, to Columbia for her treatments. That's a double or triple memory. Diane's favorite holiday was Halloween and it was with great sadness that the cancer took her on that day.

It is not unusual for a cemetery to evoke memories of loved ones buried there. When I passed Hopewell, my thoughts turned to Frank and Dorothy, our landlords when we lived on Newland hill. I thought of Aunt Addie who wasn't my aunt at all, but a wonderful woman who made the best of life in a wheelchair.

I've spent most of my life living within seven miles of where I live now. No wonder every curve, hill, and landmark made me think of the people who passed through my life, influencing me, making me the person I am today.

If we really turned back time today—not for an hour but could turn it back to a different time—it might not be the miracle we would envision. Just think, one small change in our past would bring us to an entirely different destiny. We could drive ourselves insane with a thousand *what ifs*.

When a loved one dies, they take a piece of us with them, but they also leave part of themselves behind. We are left with memories, and we are changed. Remembering good times is a way to appreciate the gift of love. A productive, happy life is based on what we were, how we cherish what we are now, and the audacity to believe the future will be filled with hope, happiness, and adventure.

November Is Alzheimer's Awareness Month

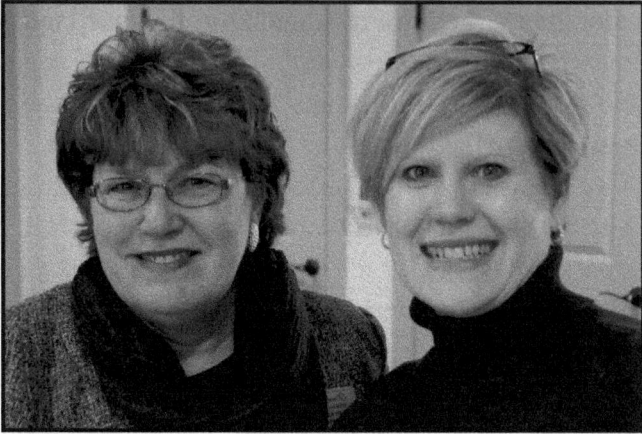

The month of November is a month of pumpkins, fall décor, Thanksgiving, and the onslaught of the Christmas season. It is also Alzheimer's Awareness Month.

I recently attended a "Coffee with Congress" at Provision Living Center in Columbia. I consider this as a "kickoff" to Alzheimer's Awareness month.

It probably should have been called Coffee with Congressional staff. Newbies to advocacy often become irate when they think they are going to talk to a member of Congress and instead talk to a staff member. I've seen perfectly capable advocates waste an opportunity to wholeheartedly share their message. Staff members are focused on what you have to say and they will share the relevant information with their boss.

In this instance, we met with three staff members. I had a great visit with Janna Worsham with Congresswoman Vicky Hartzler's office, Sarah Barfield Graff with Senator Roy Blunt's office, and Kyle Klemp with Senator Claire McCaskill's office. We talked about funding for Alzheimer's research and thanked them for their support.

We are proud of our Missouri group. Senator Blunt has requested $350 million additional funds for Alzheimer's research. That is $50 million more than our ask. Senator McCaskill is the top ranking democrat on the special committee on aging. We saw her in action at the Alzheimer's Public policy forum when she joined Chairman Susan Collins (R-Maine) to head a bipartisan hearing focusing on the financial, economic, and emotional challenges facing those with Alzheimer's disease and their families.

In addition, I wanted to thank Congresswoman Vicky Hartzler for her unwavering support for Alzheimer's research. One year when we brought a letter asking for a modest increase in Alzheimer's research, she had already sent a request for $1 billion. She also uses Facebook, Twitter, and her newsletter to create her own storm of Alzheimer's awareness. She and I connect on a personal level because we know the heartbreak of losing a loved one to dementia.

We also discussed the HOPE for Alzheimer's Act and the asset the Act would be for families dealing with the disease. The Act is a common sense approach to providing Medicare coverage for comprehensive care planning services for newly diagnosed individuals and his or her caregiver, ensure that a diagnosis and care planning are included in medical records, and to require the Department of Health and Human Services to educate providers about the benefits.

As a caregiver, I kept track of Jim's medical conditions—symptoms, diagnosis, tests run, side effects of prescription medications, and any information relative to his health. I took prints of the spreadsheet to every appointment. This kept him from being prescribed medications he couldn't take, duplication of tests, and helped me fill out all those darned forms.

What happens to the people who don't have someone to tell every specialist what others have done? The HOPE Act doesn't have a "Score" which is an indication of what it would cost the government. Somehow, I think that instead of a cost to the government, it would save patients and the government by reducing duplicated services or writing prescriptions for medicine that has already created problems.

We heard caregiver stories including a care partner who was there with his lovely wife. He told of their problems with getting a diagnosis of early-onset Alzheimer's. I shared some of my caregiving experiences. Several Greater Missouri Chapter staff and Board members were present to tell their stories and share their passion.

The meeting was informative, encouraging, and relevant. Those of us attending the Coffee with Congress left with a conviction to do everything within our power to end this horrible disease. We look forward to the day that Alzheimer's becomes a manageable disorder, or better yet, when researchers find a cure.

.

Welcome to My World

Still dressed in my PJ's and first cup of coffee in hand, I headed toward my downstairs office yesterday morning. Harold had already forewarned me that as soon as the weather was warm enough we would return to painting fence posts and rails. I was determined to get an early start on my blog.

I sat in front of my PC trying to decide if I dare jump into writing my blog post, or if I should tackle my To-Do list first. I balanced the options in my head. If I worked on my To-Do list, I would be jumping from task to task spinning my figurative wheels in an attempt to multitask my multitasks. Hours would fly past while I whittled down my list only to add more. The list has a life of its own, and it is never ending.

Blog—a firm decision. I should have done it Friday, and here it was Tuesday, so I was already four days behind. My quandary helped me decide on the title: "Welcome to My World."

I placed my fingers on the keyboard and noticed my nail polish was worn and chipped. I would have done them Monday before the Alzheimer's board meeting, but the power was out when it was time to get ready, and still out when I should have been finished. Just as I had thrown everything in the car to go to the other house to shower, the power came back on.

I typed the title, and my phone sounded an alarm. Ignore it, my left brain said. Better look at it, my right brain replied.

Curiosity won. *Hair appointment: 10 a.m.* What? Well, that's just dandy. Here it is 9:30, and I have to be dressed and in town in thirty minutes.

I abandoned my first cup of coffee and ran up the stairs knowing I'd need to be dressed in record time. Short of breath, I rushed into Harold's office to tell him the good news. I threw on clothes and a little makeup. No need fussing with my hair—that's my hairdresser's job. No need for earrings—they would only get in the way.

After getting my hair cut and styled, I made a quick trip to the grocery store. As I put the groceries in the car, I saw the box of sponsor T-shirts in the backseat. It was a perfect day to deliver them, but too warm to leave groceries in the car. Besides, it was time to get home and paint. At least my hair looked great until I put on the paint mask and pulled the elastic to the back of my head.

So, seriously, welcome to my world. But then again, I think it's everyone's world now. I don't hold the patent on crazy, busy days. Looking back on my life, it seems it has always been that way. When my kids were little, days blurred into weeks, into months, and years until they weren't little anymore. Then, Jim became more dependent on me to provide his essential care. I became immersed in caring for him and added volunteering for the Alzheimer's Association to the To-Do list.

As if working, being a caregiver, and volunteer work wasn't enough, I went back to college. How did I do it? I have no clue. I took it a day at a time. Heck, sometimes it was minute to minute.

I wonder how any of us do it. Do we take on more than humanly possible, or are we simply making the most of the time we have allotted to us? Are we doing the things we love, or are we fulfilling obligations and pushing aside what we really want to do?

The bottom line is that it's all about balance. I don't want to be the kind of person that blows off obligations, but I don't want to be the kind of person that only has time for obligations. I don't mind standing in the freezing cold to ring the bell for Salvation Army any more than sitting in the comfort of my home writing a press release for scholarships.

Variety is as important as balance. This is how I've chosen to live, so I'm sharing, not complaining. I've been blessed in so many ways and am thankful for the world I've been given. With a smile, I welcome you to my world.

Rainy Days Get Me Down

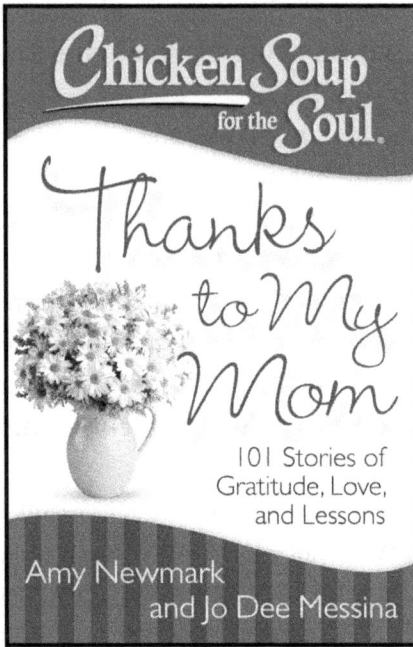

When it rains, pours, day after day, you begin to think that the earth is turning to water. All I can see from my window is rain in the yard, the fields, and every other low spot in between. The skies are a hundred shades of gray.

It's hard to let my sunny disposition shine when Mother Nature doesn't co-operate. I've been thinking too much and doing too little. I've vegged out on the couch two days straight. I watched show after show. My listless, do-nothing self became my dominant trait. It's the rain's fault.

The fall decorations were clustered together waiting for me to get up the energy to put them away. I dragged out a few of my snowmen, one of my small trees, and other Christmas odds and ends. But the bulk of the decorations are in the garage in storage tubs. Then, I turned on the tree and flipped on the TV to watch a Hallmark Christmas show. About ten minutes in, I realized I'd already seen it.

I went to bed and read until about midnight. I've had trouble sleeping since it started raining. The thinker keeps on thinking, and my normal slumber-inducing methods aren't working. For two days, the negative past swooped down on me and washed away the positive thoughts like so much driftwood.

I woke up this morning out of sorts. Testy and grumpy. At least I found the energy to tackle a few tasks.

As I sat down to write my blog post, I noticed a message on Google Plus. I called my mom to share what was written. A person on the other side of the globe wrote to comment on my special mom after reading "Under Control" in *Chicken Soup for the Soul Thanks To My Mom.*

The note said, "I was very impressed with your mother's unconditional love for you and for Jim when she tirelessly took care of him. She was still mothering you despite the fact that you have become a mother yourself. Mothering is not something perfect women do, it is something that perfects women. If she is still alive, please convey my greetings to her and tell her that someone across the globe is very proud of her."

Happily, I responded that my mom was in excellent health and would be turning eighty-nine in January. I had originally titled the story "Spicy Chicken Sandwich," but the editors at *Chicken Soup* renamed it, which is probably why they have bestsellers and I don't. It is always awesome to be in a *Chicken Soup* book. The competition is fierce.

This story didn't make it so much on my writing merit as it did the story itself. A story of how my family became my support system when I was a caregiver. They put up with me on sunny days and rainy days to help me keep Jim at home as long as possible. In "Under Control," I focused on my mom, because you can only say so much in 1,200 words. The story could have been about Jim's mom, my kids, my sisters (in-law and birth), cousins, friends, neighbors, and eventually professional caregivers.

Caregivers have a lot of rainy days. It seems that down days come in clusters.

Rain, and bad days, may seem like they are going to last forty days and forty nights. About the time you think you should get started on that Ark, the rainbow brings the promise that everything is going to be all right. Next thing you know, the sun pops through and dares those dark clouds to show their frowning gray faces.

Yep. It's still raining here in Missouri, but I've passed through the gloom and doom. I'm ready to tackle the world—tomorrow.

Letters about Alzheimer's and Coconut Oil

I checked my post office box a few days ago and was pleasantly surprised to see two handwritten missives. In today's atmosphere of mass mailings, junk mail, advertisements, and "or current occupant" mailings, it is almost mind-boggling to get one handwritten note, much less an entire letter.

The first note was from one of our Walk to End Alzheimer's sponsors. Jessica Snell and I had recently delivered T-shirts and a copy of *Broken Road: Navigating the Alzheimer's Labyrinth*, a publication of my 2014 Early Onset Alzheimer's blog posts. After thanking us for the shirts, she wrote, "It's our pleasure to support this effort. I have forwarded your book to our social workers and case managers because I thought they would find it insightful."

The other note was from a gentleman who began with "I have Alzheimer's, and I read your book." He didn't mention which book he read. In addition to the first book I compiled and edited, *Alzheimer's Anthology of Unconditional Love*, I have seven other Alzheimer's books from my blog. "My wife said I have quit talking and reading. Today I read your entire book and I will read the Bible for two years." He went on to talk about his coconut oil regimen. He said that one of the things I did not mention in my book is coconut oil and its benefits for Alzheimer's.

He is not the first person to ask why I haven't talked about the benefits of coconut oil. I never tried coconut oil on Jim, so I have no personal experience to share about this alternative treatment.

There is little scientific research on coconut oil and Alzheimer's disease. A trial was supposed to be completed in September 2015, but for some reason it has been delayed and the results are not yet available. So, basically, the jury is still out on the benefits, or a possible downside, of coconut oil therapy.

Coconut oil has its staunch supporters and anecdotal testimony. Some testimonials say their loved ones showed immediate improvement after taking daily doses of coconut oil for a short time.

Coconut oil contains more MCT (medium chain triglycerides) than any other food. MCT produces ketones, which some researchers believe can improve Alzheimer's symptoms. Some very small studies showed improved cognitive function from MCT supplements. These studies used a supplement, not coconut oil.

A cautionary tale is that the safety of coconut oil in medicinal amounts is unknown. Its impact on cholesterol levels in high dosages is in dispute. Another consideration is that just because something is "natural" doesn't mean it is safe when taken in abnormal amounts.

I know the frustration of waiting for an effective treatment for Alzheimer's and I, too, used vitamin E supplements for Jim. I did clear the dosage with his physician and told every specialist he saw that he was taking it. None saw it as a problem.

I also take a couple of supplements—CoQ10 and MegaRed for joint problems. My physician knows I take these, and I've seen tremendous benefits from taking both. I took different levels until I found the lowest dosage that provided the best results. They don't work for everyone, but I have confidence this regimen works for me.

Perhaps, it is the same with coconut oil. It may not work for everyone, but it may work for some. I do know primary caregivers will see even subtle changes in a loved one with dementia. We want the highest quality of life without causing any harm.

Once the larger studies are completed, science may come down on one side or the other in the coconut oil question. In the meantime, I would urge caution and consultation with a trusted medical professional before beginning *any* alternative treatment.

Aging Well Is All about Attitude

Have you ever noticed that some people seem old before their time? The reason some appear to be elderly could be due to physical appearance—they have wrinkles, shuffle when they walk—or more obviously they have turned into a grumpy old person.

Then, there is my mom. She will be eighty-nine next month but has apparently been dipping her toes in the fountain of youth. She is healthy, active, and beautiful.

A good attitude is a key factor toward determining whether your twilight years are enjoyable and fruitful. A poor attitude may mean you are looking for an excuse to check out from life early. You see people who struggle with the concept of retirement. It takes less effort and risk to keep on working. It isn't always people who need the money who don't retire, they may be afraid of not having enough to do or tie their self-worth to their career.

I took early retirement. I loved my job and worked hard to succeed, but deep inside, I knew it was "time." I was ready to turn the page on a new chapter—or perhaps open a new book. I faced retirement with excitement and without any regrets.

Recently, after exchanging pleasantries, a Walmart checker said she was glad her day was almost over and she could go home. "I have to work another five years before I can retire. That is if my health holds out."

I swiped my credit card and said, "My doctor said she was glad I retired while I was in good health and could enjoy it. She said so many people wait until they can't work anymore."

Retirement has been kind to me. I love waking up when I want to—at least most of the time. I choose the path to walk most days, or the comfy chair to sit in and read a book, or the TV show to watch, or the social event to attend. Oh, sometimes living with a farmer means being dragged into all kinds of projects. Guess that counts as physical exercise and saves on a gym membership.

In order to live, you must embrace life. If you live everyday letting other people bring you down, you find yourself marking time, instead of making the most of it. Each day is a blessing. We never know what tomorrow, or the next hour, might bring. We choose to live, or we choose to endure a living death.

As we age, we are prone to developing medical conditions. Some of these can be brought on by lifestyle, genetics, environment, or a combination of all three. Alzheimer's is one of the most dreaded conditions for the elderly. It is not a normal part of aging, but aging is the number one risk factor.

Researchers found a link between being negative about old age and developing Alzheimer's disease. The Baltimore Longitudinal Study of Aging conducted a thirty-year study on aging. Later in the study, they used scans to track the size of the participants' hippocampus, which is primarily associated with memory and spatial navigation. The people who began the study with a negative outlook on aging had greater size reduction of the hippocampus than their more positive counterparts. Autopsies found negative people had significantly more plaques and tangles, the hallmarks of Alzheimer's disease.

That's good news for those of us who see the up side of aging. We look forward to doing our own thing and taking advantage of those senior discounts. Who would have ever thought attitude could be so darned healthy?

It helps to put setbacks and failures in perspective. One thing is sure in life—even during the darkest hours, a lot of people in this world are facing greater hardships than I have ever known.

Hey, life is hard. It can be a lot harder for some than others, but giving up is not an option. It is heartening to see people who rise above adversity and take control of their own destiny.

It's all about attitude. You're only as old as your attitude lets you be. If you don't believe me, talk to my mom.

Merry, or not so Merry?

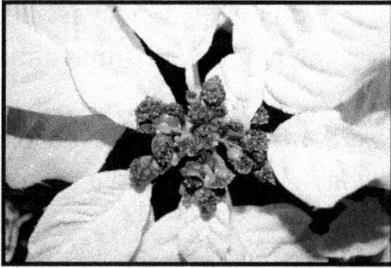

Yesterday, I met the un-merriest checker *ever* at Walmart in Columbia. The light was lit to indicate the lane was open, so Harold and I put our items on the belt. We could see the checker who was supposed to be on duty, deep in conversation with another woman. Finally, she spotted us, as we patiently waited for someone to ring up our purchases.

She sauntered over, not saying a word or even giving a hint of a smile, and picked up the items, one by one, scanning. The total came up; she glared and nodded toward the credit card machine. I scanned the card, and she handed me the receipt. Then, she begrudgingly murmured, "Thank you," beneath her breath. Anyway, she said something that ended in "you." I wouldn't a hundred percent swear the first word was "thank."

"Wow! She was rude," I said as soon as I was out of earshot. Yes, maybe I should have challenged her to her face, but I'm not passive-aggressive so I didn't say it loud enough for her to overhear.

I know she had a voice because we interrupted her conversation. I don't know what her problem was. She certainly wouldn't be in contention for employee of the month.

It was disconcerting to see someone act that way in a retail business that offers a high level of customer service, but some people just don't do holidays well. People who have suffered a tragedy at Christmas time often endure rather than enjoy.

Holiday cheer and noise don't bode well for people with dementia. A lot of holiday chaos can send a person with Alzheimer's into a tailspin.

Here are a few suggestions to make the holidays easier if you have a loved one with dementia:

1. Keep the celebrations simple. It is much better to have an intimate dinner than a huge family gathering. If it's too hard for you to host the holiday celebration, ask someone else to host it.
2. Be kind to yourself! If it's too much to maintain all the traditions of holidays past, choose the ones that mean the most. Especially, if they are ones you can let your loved one share with you. Can your loved one ice the Christmas cookies?
3. Take time for yourself. Find a few moments to indulge yourself. You could go to a Christmas program, schedule a relaxing massage, or go to a movie with a friend.

The person who can make your Christmas merry is you. Everyone else can jump through hoops trying to make it happen, but merriness doesn't come from Walmart, it comes from the heart. You will find those who give you the gift of friendship, kindness, and love will help bring joy to your holiday.

Don't let anyone steal your joy or cast guilt on you for not being able to do all that you did in the past. Fill the holidays with peace.

If you happen to go into the Columbia Walmart and see a checker with a scowl on her face and a Grinch in her heart, tell her I said, "Merry Christmas!" She probably needs all the encouragement and cheer she can get.

Alzheimer's War: A New Hope

At our family celebration, the day after Christmas, my grandson opened his *Star Wars* Lego's. He is fascinated with all things *Star Wars*.

"Has he seen the new *Star Wars* movie," I asked his dad.

"No, he hasn't," Rob replied.

I mentioned a photo posted on Facebook showing people lined up in front of a movie theater to see the original *Star Wars* in 1977. The caption read, "Your grandparents lined up to see the first *Star Wars*."

"I remember when your dad and I took you and Eric to see *Star Wars*. We went to the drive-in to see it and you both fell asleep." Of course, drive-in movies didn't start until after dark and five- and seven-year-olds were up past their bedtimes. So, Jim and I were the only ones to see the entire movie.

"I don't even remember it," Rob said. He didn't remember getting the toys for Christmas either: R2D2 and C3PO.

Of course, at the time, we thought there would only be one *Star Wars* movie. Instead, it was the series of movies that just kept on giving, and in 2015 gave again. What I didn't know was that due to the prequels, the original *Star Wars* movie's name was changed to *Star Wars Episode IV A New Hope*.

It seems odd that an original movie in a series would be renamed, "A New Hope." I find that intriguing for life as well. We all face so much adversity living from day to day that we could use a little bit of "new" hope to keep us going.

When dealing with Alzheimer's, we may have years of sorrow, months of endurance, weeks of despair, and days of joy, but through it all, we never give up hope. With Alzheimer's, hope may be simply hoping for a good day, hoping that the family pulls together, and hope there is something way better than this world. Hope for a miracle burrows deep within our hearts, and that the cure will be discovered in time to save our loved ones.

Now, we have a new hope. We have hope that this disease will be stamped out in our lifetime. Finally, our nation is pulling together to fund research in an unprecedented amount. We have declared war on Alzheimer's.

On December 22, Harry Johns, CEO of the Alzheimer's Association, said, "As we celebrate this momentum for our cause, we are, of course, deeply appreciative of our champions in Congress, members from both parties, who have made the advances we need much more likely with the historic funding increase announced last week. They have provided unprecedented leadership that will ultimately make a difference in millions and millions of lives."

I'll be making my sixteenth consecutive trip to the Alzheimer's Advocacy Forum in April to help celebrate this new hope. Yes, an increase in funding is a great victory but our work isn't done, and it won't be, until Alzheimer's is a curable disease.

A cure has been my hope for many, many years. My new hope is that someday I'll go to D.C. and won't have anything on my agenda except sight-seeing. Until then, I'll wear my purple sash and continue to fight the war against Alzheimer's.

Alzheimer's Communication: The Sounds of Silence

Simon and Garfunkel's song "The Sounds of Silence" always touched me. When I heard the cover performed by Disturbed, it made me hear the lyrics in a different context—a more urgent one.

The same words performed in a different manner brought a new dimension to the song and made me pay attention to parts of it that previously blended into the background.

The haunting lyrics of "The Sounds of Silence" make me think of how Jim's voice was silenced with aphasia during his years with dementia. His problems began with a few jumbled words until his voice was stilled except for an occasional word. When a spoken word broke through the boundary of silence, it was as treasured as a rare jewel.

Mostly, Jim learned to talk without speaking, without words. His mannerisms became the clues that told us of his needs. His eyes communicated his pleasure, pain, joy, confusion, and a myriad of emotions.

Jim always said he knew me better than I knew myself, and I believe that was the key to our communication. Instinctively, he knew how to get his point across to me.

Communicating with a loved one who has Alzheimer's requires some thought. When you consider that only about seven percent of communication is from words, it opens many possibilities.

1. Speak in simple, straightforward sentences and give only one instruction at a time. When I asked Jim to do two things in one sentence, he only reacted to the second request.
2. Patience is your friend! Allow time for a response. Don't expect a quick response, or even an appropriate one.
3. Use body language to make your point. Your loved one will understand tone of voice and body language long beyond the time when they understand your words. Point, demonstrate, or use props. Also, watch your loved one's body language. Restlessness, irritability, and other physical symptoms will alert you to their distress.
4. Validate the emotions you see and hear. Their reaction to something might be completely different from yours, or even what you would expect theirs to be. They may re-live grief over and over, or may not acknowledge there is anything to grieve even when a close relative dies.

Throughout life, we communicate—from a baby's cry, parenting, learning in school, to our last profound words. Life is more complicated and confusing when we lose our lifelong ability to communicate effectively.

Communication isn't easy when your loved one has dementia, but putting in the effort to keep the lines of communication open will help your loved one and you maintain a happier relationship. Loving words, hugs, and smiles will convey your deepest feelings. When you listen with your heart, the sounds of silence will tell you everything you need to know.

Alzheimer's Anthology of Unconditional Love

Edited by L. S. Fisher

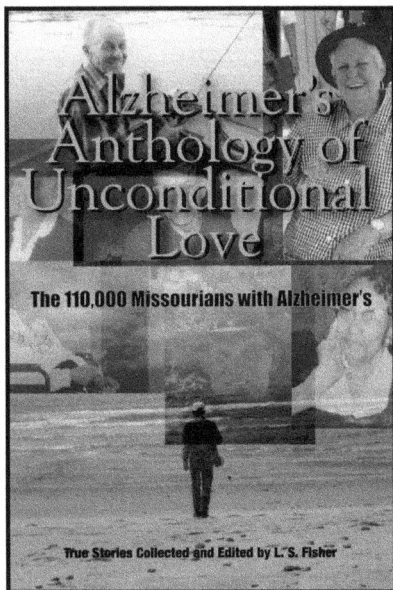

Mozark Press
PO Box 1746
Sedalia, MO 65302

www.MozarkPress.com
www.lsfisher.com

Early Onset Blog: Essays from an Online Journal

By L. S. Fisher

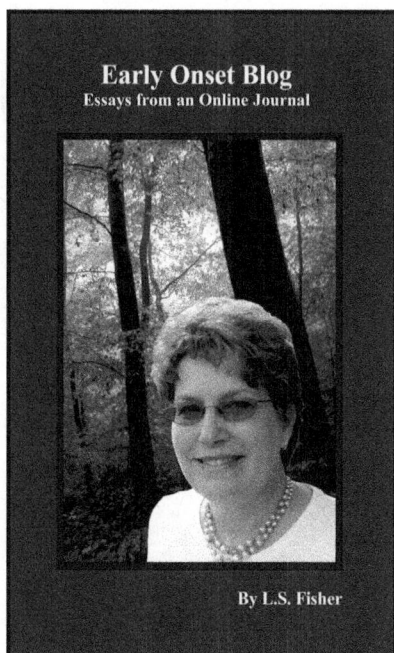

Mozark Press
PO Box 1746
Sedalia, MO 65302

www.MozarkPress.com
www.lsfisher.com

Early Onset Blog: The Friendship Connection
&
Other Essays

By L. S. Fisher

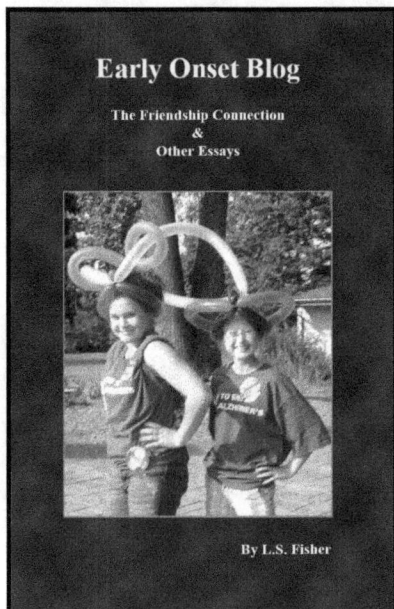

Mozark Press
PO Box 1746
Sedalia, MO 65302

www.MozarkPress.com
www.lsfisher.com

Early Onset Alzheimer's
Encourage, Inspire, and Inform

By L. S. Fisher

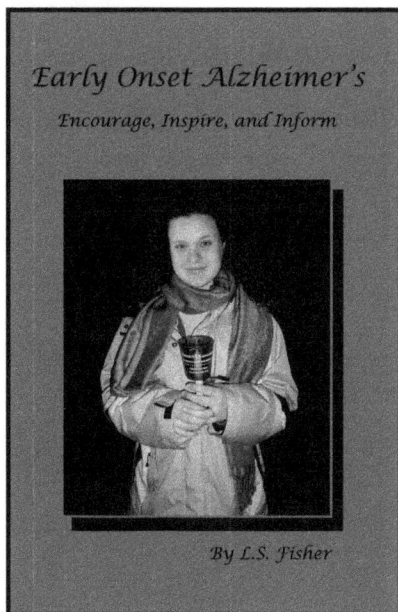

Mozark Press
PO Box 1746
Sedalia, MO 65302

www.MozarkPress.com
www.lsfisher.com

Early Onset Alzheimer's
My Recollections, Our Memories

By L. S. Fisher

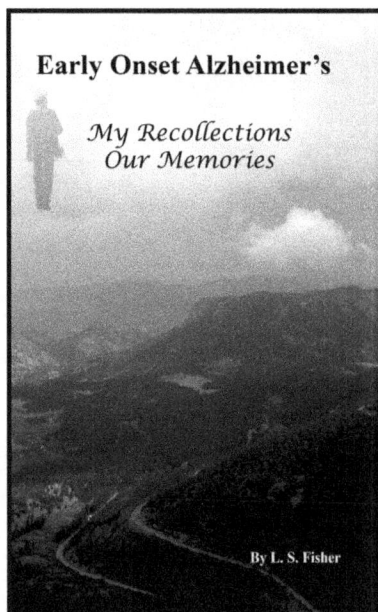

Mozark Press
PO Box 1746
Sedalia, MO 65302

www.MozarkPress.com
www.lsfisher.com

Focus on the Positive
Inspire, Encourage, and Inform

By L. S. Fisher

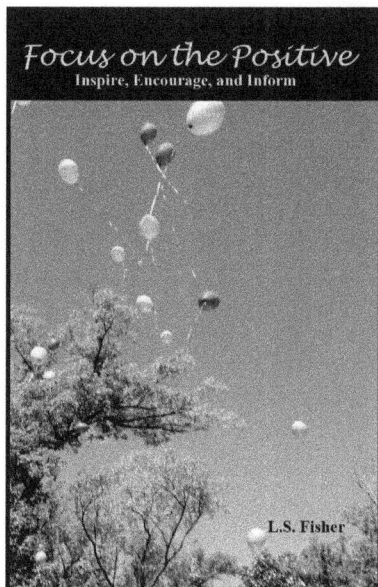

Mozark Press
PO Box 1746
Sedalia, MO 65302

www.MozarkPress.com
www.lsfisher.com

Garden of Hope
Growing Alzheimer's Awareness

By L. S. Fisher

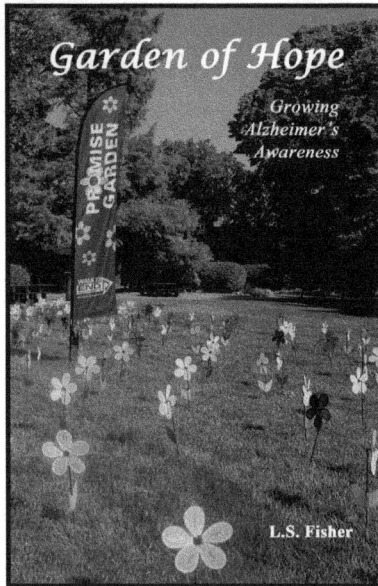

Mozark Press
PO Box 1746
Sedalia, MO 65302

www.MozarkPress.com
www.lsfisher.com

The Broken Road
Navigating the Alzheimer's Labyrinth

By L. S. Fisher

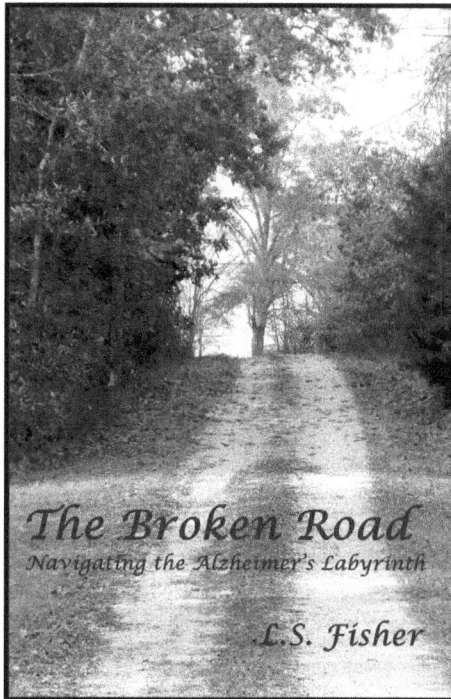

Mozark Press
PO Box 1746
Sedalia, MO 65302

www.MozarkPress.com
www.lsfisher.com

Memory Talk

Linda Fisher
Alzheimer's Speaker

Author and Editor
of
Alzheimer's Anthology of Unconditional Love

Linda is a longtime Alzheimer's Association volunteer and advocate. She speaks from her personal experience as a primary caregiver for her husband who lived with early onset dementia for ten years. She will speak to your group or organization about Alzheimer's or writing life stories. Choose from the following presentations, or request a different Alzheimer's or writing topic:

Writing as Therapy: Rocks and Pebbles

Where are your real life stories? Learn how to reconnect with the pebbles of your life and how writing these stories can be therapeutic. Discover slice-of-life moments that only you know. Suitable for senior adult writing groups, caregivers, and support groups.

Alzheimer's Voices of Experience

Learn about Alzheimer's from short excerpts of the heartfelt stories collected in *Alzheimer's Anthology of Unconditional Love*. These true stories allow you to glimpse the lives of real people who have embarked upon an unwilling journey into the world of dementia. This presentation gives a face and voice to the statistics of a baffling disease. Suitable for nursing home staff, caregivers, Alzheimer's staff and volunteers, civic organizations, and people who want to know more about dementia.

Alzheimer's Can Happen at Any Age

A PowerPoint presentation that focuses on raising awareness that Alzheimer's is a neurological brain disease and not a normal part of aging. Suitable for nursing home staff, caregivers, Alzheimer's staff and volunteers, civic organizations, and people who want to know more about dementia.

Alzheimer's Caregivers: Survive and Thrive

A workshop to develop caregiver coping skills. Linda speaks from her personal experience as a primary caregiver for her husband who lived with early onset dementia for ten years. Suitable for caregivers.

Alzheimer's Caregiver Stress

A PowerPoint presentation covering signs of stress and stress management techniques. Linda learned coping skills from her personal experience as a primary caregiver for her husband. Suitable for caregivers and support groups.

Alzheimer's Communication: Hear their Voices

A presentation to develop communication skills. Linda draws on her experience as the primary caregiver for her husband and his difficulty communicating due to aphasia. Suitable for nursing home staff, caregivers, volunteers, and civic organizations.

Caregiver Emotions

This one-hour seminar will help you identify seven caregiver emotions and develop strategies to cope with the emotional rollercoaster. This presentation focuses on the Alzheimer's caregiver, but care partners of other serious ailments can benefit from this program.

To schedule a presentation:

Email: lfisher@lsfisher.com

From the Author

My therapist is on call twenty-four hours a day. Some of my most successful sessions occur in the middle of the night when I'm comfortable in my pajamas. I grab a pen and paper or fire up my laptop and write through my worries, hurt, or anger.

I began journaling when I was twelve years old, and knew that writing helped me collect my thoughts and look at my problems more objectively. After I married and began to raise a family, I put away my journals except for an occasional travel log.

When my husband Jim developed dementia at forty-nine, I felt the need to write again. Through the ten years of Jim's dementia, I kept a detailed journal, mostly on tape. When I later transcribed the tapes, I re-discovered a wealth of information to help me heal.

Just like talking to a therapist, writing eased me through the emotionally draining decade of Jim's illness. The power of the pen healed my spirit.

Gathering and editing stories for *Alzheimer's Anthology of Unconditional Love* gave me purpose after Jim's death. I'm still working on a memoir and hope these stories can help others along their journeys. My love of writing complements my volunteer work and helps me focus on the power of positive thinking and action.

L. S. Fisher lives, works, and writes in Sedalia, MO. The greatest tragedy in her life led to her greatest accomplishments. If her husband had not developed dementia, she would have spent her days working and her evenings at home. Instead, she has been recognized locally, statewide, and nationally for her Alzheimer's Association volunteer work.

Website: www.lsfisher.com
Blog: http://earlyonset.blogspot.com

Essay originally published in *Bylines 2010 Writer's Desk Calendar*, Snowflake Press, www.bylinescalendar.com

MoZARK PRESS

Sedalia, Missouri

Mozark Press is a small publishing company in central Missouri dedicated to producing quality paperback books. We will publish short story collections, inspirational works, anthologies, general fiction, and non-fiction. Mozark Press plans to publish 1-5 new books per year that meet our standards. We expect manuscripts to be polished and error-free when submitted. Contact us if you want to see your work in print, but haven't been successful with a major publishing company. Maybe you have considered self-publishing, but do not have the time or know-how to do it yourself. We've been there, done that, and wouldn't wish it on anyone.

We are interested in new or established authors. Mozark Press will partner with our authors. We will provide a complimentary author webpage for one year. We won't ask you to sign a long-term contract.

We do not accept unsolicited manuscripts. If you have a completed manuscript, you would like us to consider, send a query letter to:

Publisher@mozarkpress.com

www.ingramcontent.com/pod-product-compliance
Lightning Source LLC
Chambersburg PA
CBHW070809050426
42452CB00011B/1956